D1667590

THIEVERY:
Catholic Church
EXPOSED!

BY

LES COCHRAN

**THORN BIRD
PUBLICATIONS**

Published by
Thorn Bird Publications
Weaverville, NC 28787

Copyright © 2019 by Les Cochran

All rights reserved.

This book is a documentary based on real events.
The book incorporates approved works from third parties,
and modified works in accordance with "fair use" guidelines.
No part of this publication may be reproduced or transmitted in any
form or by any means, electronic or mechanical, including
photocopy, recording, or any information storage and
retrieval system, without permission in writing
from the copyright owner.

ISBN: 978-0-578-52352-1

First Edition
September 2019

Foreword

Documentaries are often the results of years of thought, personal experience, revenge to get even, or a deep-seated research mission to set the record straight. None of these motives generated the spark for writing *THIEVERY: Catholic Church EXPOSED!*

I'd never given thought to the internal operation of the Catholic Church. I'm not Catholic. I didn't have a score to even. Nor did I have a burning passion to reveal the sins of the Church.

So, why then, did I undertake this investigative project?

I've been asked this question countless times. The answer is simple, it was a happenstance event.

I was at an art festival in Detroit promoting my historical fiction series "Detroit Thorn Birds Defy Mafia." Highlighting one of the episodes, I gave an example of money laundering between the mafia and the Catholic Church. A young man in the group quickly responded, "You ought to check out the crooks in the Catholic Church today!"

After completing the book sale, I looked up and the young man was gone, but his comment was not forgotten. Going over my notes a week or so later, "Check out the crooks..." caught my eye, so I googled "crooks, thievery, Catholic Church."

I couldn't believe my eyes; Michigan was not the only state where criminal activity was taking place. I researched back to 2002, when the pedophile scandal exploded, and found no one had undertaken a comprehensive investigation of "thievery" in the Catholic Church. My latent research tendencies sprang into action — I was back in my old academic arena — digging, probing, and googling to the nth degree.

Michael W. Ryan's publication, *NONFEASANCE: The Remarkable Failure of the Catholic Church to Protect Its Primary Source of*

Income, published in 2011, detailed corrective actions to be taken by priests and bishops. Yet, reported cases of embezzlement, fraud, and theft continued to grow.

Smaller, segmented research studies have been published, but *THIEVERY* is the first comprehensive investigation of financial mismanagement in the Catholic Church. Based upon an analysis of ninety-seven cases, reported from 2002 to 2018, it utilizes actual news stories to portray illegal and unethical actions taken by bishops, priests, and others associated with the Church.

Les Cochran

Table of Contents

Preface
THE SEVENTH COMMANDMENT:
Do Not Steal — Act Justly*

Have you ever taken property belonging to another person without their permission?

We are called to respect people and their possessions. The Seventh Commandment forbids theft or stealing, the taking of someone's property or money "against the reasonable will of the owner." Theft includes not just robbery, but also actions such as embezzlement, computer theft, fraud, identity theft, counterfeit money, copyright violations, pirating of music or computer software, mail scams or other type of scams.

We should not steal from one another, pay unjust wages, cheat in our business dealings, or exploit the weaknesses of others to make money. Our promises should be honored, and our contracts kept, to the extent that they are morally just. We should pay our just debts and fulfill our obligations to which we freely commit ourselves. The government has the right and the duty to enact laws to protect the legitimate ownership of money and property and to protect people from theft and injury. A violation of this Commandment requires reparation and the restitution of the stolen property

To help us keep this Commandment "we need to acquire the virtues of moderation in our possessions, justice in our treatment of others, respect for their human dignity, and solidarity with all peoples. Moderation curbs our attachment to worldly goods and restrains our appetite for consumerism. Justice helps us respect our neighbor's rights and be interested in their well-being. Solidarity opens our hearts to identifying with the whole human family, reminding us of our common humanity" *(USCCA, p. 419).

We do NOT live in isolation. We are social beings who live in relationship with others, such as our spouse, children, family, friends, neighbors, co-workers, Parish, community, and other cultures to which we belong.

U. S. Catholic Catechism for Adults, Ch. 31.

There are roughly 37,000 Catholic priests in the United States — the vast number of them have dedicated their lives to God and the church community — and thousands more church members who've worked tirelessly behind the scenes to support their religion. This documentary is not about them; nor is it "priest bashing."

It's about those priests, employees, and laity who've failed to fulfill their obligations and responsibilities. Worse yet, some schemed, connived, and lied to hide their thievery. It concerns the unethical behavior of bishops and other church officials who *chose* not to confront these individuals; who instead, *chose* to hide their misdeeds, and unscrupulously schemed, connived, and lied — which in fact, led to more stealing and embezzlement, more negative press, and added to the current financial crisis.

CHAPTER ONE
The Untold Story

For the early part of the 21st Century, the sex abuse scandal dominated comment about the Catholic Church. And rightfully so! Thousands of priests imposed their will upon innocent children with no regard for their prey or their own priesthood oath! There's no doubt the sex abuse scandal deserves the attention it received.

But these priests were not the only ones engaged in deviant behavior, and sex abuse was not the Church's only form of criminality; thousands of priests and staff members were embezzling and stealing, giving root to the thievery scandal.

While not directly involved in the scams, complex schemes, and other forms of financial misconduct, several bishops were lax in their supervision of priests. Countless priests also failed to fulfill their duties; thereby, allowing staff and laity members of the parish to engage in unethical behavior. It was as if no morality or ethics existed among many of those in charge.

Collection plate and other donations were commandeered for their own pleasures.

As their devious actions were eventually uncovered, members of the effected parishes remained in denial; they couldn't believe — didn't want to believe — these presumed saintly men, entrusted employees, and parish volunteers had betrayed them. The local media "walked gingerly" in reporting their transgressions. Occasionally a case would reach the state or regional level, but it typically ended there. If a story had a bizarre twist, it might gain national attention, only to quickly fall off the radar screen, for *thievery paled in comparison to sex abuse!*

***

Priestly thievery and that of the laity, however, had not yet been revealed in its entirety. A step back in history offers a glimpse into the handling of these larcenous issues. Fact is, rumors and innuendos about the handling of donations have long plagued the Catholic Church.

Over the years, Church leaders acted minimally to remedy the issue. On November 27, 1983, bishops passed a revised Code of Canon Law, to make clear the responsibilities of bishops and administrators. Canon 1284 stated:

All administrators are to perform their duties with the diligence of a "good householder." The bishop can delegate authority, but not responsibility. He has the duty to ensure no abuses exist in the administration of the churches within the diocese. "Every pastor is required" to appoint a committee of lay members to monitor spending priorities and manage the parish's money.

With little deviation, parishes continued their careless ways of dealing with financial matters. Although many parish finance councils were formed, often they operated ineffectively, simply functioning as paper councils that did little more than approve whatever was submitted by the pastor. Often, bishops failed to follow up on the actions of priests to ensure they had complied with the mandate.

***

In 1995, the United States Conference of Catholic Bishops (USCCB) addressed the issue again releasing a document called, "Diocesan Internal Controls: A Framework" (12). The 35-page document delineated specific steps and procedures to be followed in all areas of financial management, including:

- How to establish and effectively use internal controls,
- Roles and responsibilities for all personnel from the bishop down and all committees,
- The importance of using an external auditor,
- Control over assets, contributions, and step-by-step recordkeeping controls,
- Guidelines for internal control, and
- Types of fraud, how to detect it, and handle related issues.

The document sounded like the ultimate solution, but it did little to curtail financial mismanagement. Like other USCCB statements, *it contained a series of recommendations, NOT mandates.* Bishops and pastors were free to follow the rules or not. Even when official diocesan policy required their implementation, action taken by pastors at the parish level was often hit or miss.

Rumors persisted and financial improprieties continued.

***

The bishops' actions in 1983 and 1995 were little more than window-dressing. Cases continued to appear across the country, as illustrated by the sampling found at "Church Embezzlement Case Histories," at www.churchsecurity.info:

1990	Oshkosh, WI	Priest sentenced to six months in jail and three years of probation for stealing $45,000 from donations.
1990	Providence, RI	Former pastor indicted for skimming $200,000 from collections and embezzling funds from parish accounts.
1990	Providence, RI	In an unrelated case, church employee accused of embezzling $58,000 from parish funds.
1992	Los Angeles, CA	Priest, who insisted on handling all funds, accused of embezzling $60,000 in collection monies.
1993	Dallas, TX	Church secretary admitted to pocketing $240,000 from plates.
1996	Ottawa, OH	Woman sentenced to two years for stealing more than $400,000 from collections to fund her lavish lifestyle.
1998	Providence, RI	Priest pleaded no contest to embezzling $90,000 from members of the Church.
1998	Pittsburgh, PA	Priest admitted to skimming over $1,350,000 over twenty-six years from collection plates, then committed suicide.
1999	Pittsburgh, PA	Church secretary avoided prison for helping priest steal $25,000; priest died before trial.
1999	Santa Rosa, CA	After assuring parishioners he would deal openly with priest misconduct, the bishop hushed-up theft admitted to by a priest.

In another case in 1998, in the Diocese of Pittsburgh, Michael W. Ryan (39) noted that the bishop labeled thievery as "an aberration." Pointing out to the press that the parishes in the diocese were audited every three years.

Ryan goes on to report USCCB members were unwilling to address their procedures dealt only with the amount of documented money. The most prevalent means of stealing was taking the money directly from the offering plate — before it was recorded.

Ryan also noted, "I have access to only a fraction of those cases, i.e., those that received significant publicity in the media; a sizable research staff would be required to keep tabs on every local newspaper. Diocesan files no doubt contain records of many embezzlement cases that were never reported in the media."

Following a series of communications Ryan had with USCCB leaders during the 1990s regarding the need for uniformly secure procedures for handling Sunday collections (the most theft-prone area), a USCCB representative notified him in December 1999. He stated Canon Law prohibited USCCB from mandating the way collection funds are handled within individual dioceses.

That claim precipitated a review of Canon Law in which Ryan eventually determined the USCCB was specifically authorized to "Draw up rules regarding collections, which must be observed by all." Under provisions of Canon 455, the issuance of general decrees, if approved by two-thirds of its members, apply Conference-wide.

Nevertheless, following a period of silence from USCCB, Ryan recalled in December of 2001, the new President of USCCB responded to him with another letter on the topic, stating, "I concur with the expressions of my predecessors."

The positions obstinately held by USCCB reinforced well-established views of the Church regarding the seemingly unlimited autonomy of individual bishops.

***

As illustrated by these examples, questions of accountability and transparency had generated long-standing issues inside the Catholic Church. While influenced by numerous forces, three underlying concepts shaped most of the dialogue.

First, and foremost, the Catholic Church is a "faith-based" organization. As such, the Church's core values of trust and honesty drive its operation, just as trust and honesty drives its religious mission. The two segments have been viewed as one, inseparable.

Its leaders commit to the highest ethical standards — they've lived their lives in a certain way and refrained from behaviors that might, in any way, detract from *their* defined obligations. They preach pure righteousness and purportedly represent standards well above the ways of mere mortals. They work in an environment of trust; they trust others and expect others to trust them.

Conceptually, a "faith-based" organization is workable. It sounds good, too, but in today's world, maintaining this narrow definition places the financial stability of the Church at risk. Fact is a significant number of people are not trustworthy. Without checks and balances, there are no controls.

Second, the Church often lacks sufficient internal financial controls, particularly at the parish level. The upper level of the Catholic Church is centralized under the Pope. The administrative organization at the bishop's level is highly decentralized. Parishes have far-ranging autonomy. Dioceses exercise uneven regulatory oversight over parishes. Whenever there is an issue, the buck stops with the bishop — no questions are asked beyond that point, and, seemingly, all too often issues are buried.

Another difficulty is the span of control.

The general philosophy of the Church is to provide a broad range of freedom for the parish. While this provides considerable latitude at the priest level, it opens the door for various forms of mismanagement.

A typical business model suggests a maximum of ten to twelve individuals being supervised by one person. A bishop and his staff may supervise hundreds of priests, leaving the door open to unethical actions. In the Archdioceses of Detroit, for example, the Archbishop is responsible for over two hundred and fifty parishes and even a greater number of priests. Written reports and audits are helpful, but they can't fully replace one-on-one personal contact.

Third, financial matters are often kept inside the Church and when indiscretions occur, they are often buried. How money is handled in the Catholic Church has long been an issue within the parishes and dioceses. Rumors, criticisms, condemnations, and complaints have prevailed throughout the years. Yet, for centuries, the closed, hierarchical system has simply resolved the question of thievery in its own way (or not) and closed the door; thereby, limiting the extent to which real fact-finding might occur.

Essentially the internal process is one of handling *our own* business using *our own* standards and *our own* means of operation. Such an approach requires *every individual* to be honest and truthful; otherwise, it's like having the "fox inside the chicken house" and undermines the Catholic canon of faith.

For most organizations, it's common practice to keep routine infractions and low level, unethical behavior in-house; but when criminal action is involved, the rules change, and the laws of the land prevail. Not so across-the-board in the Church; it's often guided by *what's in the best interest* of the Church.

While "faith" serves as the essential component of any religion, a "faith-based" organization without controls fails to manage finances. The adage — *money corrupts* — is as true in the Church as it is in other segments of society. By not dealing effectively with issues of embezzlement and related crimes, the Church has done a disservice to its parishioners, its pastoral employees, and volunteers entrusted to accomplish its purposes.

✻✻✻

As straightforward as it may seem to bring about change, these issues are woven deep into the culture of the Church. Analysts agree, the chances of significant change occurring are unlikely. They've stressed it would take a monumental event or series of actions, much like what happened with the sex abuse scandal, to shake the financial hierarchical structure of the Church. Even then, this challenge would eventually require Church officials to make dramatic changes in how monetary matters are handled.

But history suggests the impetus for change will not come from the Church. No doubt, most of the individuals within the hierarchical structure are honest, law-abiding people. Still, the "trusting" culture continues to present opportunities for misconduct. Pope Francis has addressed the issue, but his voice is infrequent. The opportunity for crime is present every day.

Historical evidence also dictates a transformation will not come from the membership. Rumors of financial improprieties have persisted for centuries; yet, many Catholics are complacent with this and see it as a way of life. They're unwilling to speak out in a forceful way or rally together to insist upon reform. For the membership to be a real force in bringing about change, it's apparent Catholics would need to do more than voice their dismay. They'd have to take substantive action to capture the attention of Vatican officials and openly express their unwillingness to accept any form of financial misconduct by using their last alternative — *withholding donations.*

Without this type of bold action, the final hope is that mainstream media would weigh into the fray. Based upon recent events, that's a possibility, but even then, it would require a relentless, intense, and ongoing campaign. The media would have to step up and hammer the *thievery scandal* with the same tone and vigor as applied to the *sex abuse scandal.*

***

The exposure of the sex abuse scandal in 2002 gave new meaning to the secrets hidden in the Church. One of the byproducts of the scandal included a greater focus on financial transparency and accountability. And, with that, new light was shed on thievery; as a story — it can't be ignored, in its own right — the thievery scandal unfolded with much less fanfare.

THIEVERY was envisioned to focus attention on the amount of stealing, embezzlement, and fraud in the Church. It could be labeled the Church's second greatest scandal.

In reporting on the thievery scandal, the primary purposes of *THIEVERY* are to:

- Describe various forms of mismanagement perpetrated by unethical priests and staff members,

- Utilize actual news stories to convey the unprincipled actions of priests, church employees, and volunteers,

- Delineate how officials have allowed a small segment within the ranks of the Church to define public opinion about priests and related workers,

- Portray the disreputable behavior of some of those responsible for leadership in the Church,

- Illustrate how the "faith-based" structure facilitates thievery in the Church,

- Convey the depraved inaction of some bishops to hide thievery,

- Demonstrate the unwillingness of the Church to hold bishops and priests accountable for their actions, and

- Convey a sense of urgency for the Church to take corrective action.

THIEVERY is based on ninety-seven news stories uncovered through a comprehensive assessment of legal cases, newspaper stories, and articles reported from 2002 to 2018. Due to the plethora of cases found involving illicit financial activities in the Church, a $100,000 threshold was used for inclusion in the study. Examples of these stories are referred to in the text as "notable cases."

Collectively, the cases had a direct financial impact on the Church of more than $53 million, with millions more missing and still unaccounted for. The cases occurred in over half of the states — Michigan leading the way with seventeen, followed by sixteen in

Ohio, thirteen in Pennsylvania, and ten each in New York and Wisconsin.

Starting with 2002, when the sex abuse scandal erupted, four key words — *thievery, embezzlement, Catholic priests* — were used to conduct exhaustive computer searches until the last entry for each year was evaluated, and then probing again, to follow each lead to its conclusion.

The cases highlighted in the following chapters illustrate various ways in which the purposes of parishioners were NOT honored. Sometimes it was embezzlement by a priest, then it was a secretary, or a deacon. Still, other cases pointed to the trickle-down impact of the Church's "faith-based" organizational philosophy, where it was possible for unethical behavior to be *masked by the level of trust* given to a person.

CHAPTER TWO
A Trickle Becomes a Stream
2002-2007

While the sex abuse scandal created a worldwide tsunami of public comment, in the early part of the 21st century the thievery scandal grew in its own stream of news stories. Catholic thievery cases appeared in small communities like Keystone Heights, Florida, and Allentown, Pennsylvania, and big cities — Baltimore, Chicago, and New York City. These cases, along with an outbreak of large, attention-getting stories are highlighted in this chapter.

To provide a sense of this evolution, the total dollar impact of each year is shown in the black columns below. While the dollar amounts are relatively small, the increase of 700 percent in 2003, and then a 250 percent increase from 2003 to 2004 gave a clear signal to what was likely to occur in the future.

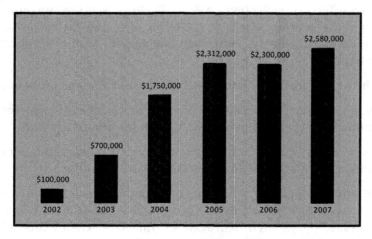

Chart 2 — A Trickle Becomes a Stream

***

Catholic Sentinel
January 10, 2002

Archdiocese Rooting Out Embezzlement*
By Ed Langlois

A sweep of rigorous financial reviews has uncovered embezzlement schemes at four Catholic parishes in western Oregon. The thefts, apparently carried off by bookkeepers and business managers, total about $280,000. District attorneys are prosecuting the cases, and parish funds are being restored through restitution and insurance.

"We have a no-tolerance policy," says Leonard Vuylsteke, director of financial services for the Archdiocese of Portland.

Amounts stolen ranged from $1,200 at one parish to $190,000 at another.

"The reason we are finding this stuff now is that the archdiocese created the financial review committee," says Vuylsteke.

"One of the things we hammer away at is internal controls over offertory collection. After offertory is taken up now, you'll see several people go to the sacristy and the money is locked up. It's always more than one person. That never used to happen."

The Archdiocese of Portland is far from alone in the problem.

In the past six years, Catholic dioceses and parishes across the nation have reported at least $3 million in embezzled funds.

Dioceses in Texas, New York and Virginia were hit with bookkeeper theft that cost a total of about $2 million.

"Fraud is happening everywhere around the country, and it is not just at corporations. Unfortunately, the church is not immune," says Ken Korotky of the U.S. Conference of Catholic Bishops' Office of Finance and Accounting Services.

*Reprinted with permission of the *Catholic Sentinel.*

Commentary: Steps taken by the Archdiocese of Portland illustrates the type of action beginning to occur. With few cases being reported, there was little understanding of the scope of the thievery problem.

***

Gainesville.com
August 23, 2003

Keystone Congregation Looks to Begin the Healing Process*

KEYSTONE HEIGHTS, FL — According to *Gainesville.com*, a Gainesville area priest will be leading the effort to help the St. William Catholic Church congregation heal after learning that their former pastor was leading a secret family life and may have embezzled hundreds of thousands of dollars from them.

Reported by *Gainesville.com*, Bishop Victor Galeone told the congregation that their former priest, Moises B. Palaroan, had a secret family life in the Philippines and may have embezzled $400,000 from the church and its members to support that life.

This weekend the Rev. Mike Williams will take over as the new priest and begin meeting with members as part of what is expected to be a long healing process.
*Reprinted in accordance with "fair use" guidelines.

Commentary: The diocese conducted an audit at each church once every four years or anytime a pastor departed. The investigators pointed out that Palaroan directed a church secretary to alter the Church's books and make unauthorized checks to him. He also is accused of borrowing as much as $100,000 from parishioners, who thought the money was going to help pay for medical costs for Palaroan's relatives in the Philippines. Instead, he sent the money to a woman with whom he had three children who were in their late teens and early 20s.

Since the Catholic Church requires priest celibacy and prohibits them from marrying, parishioners expressed their embarrassment and were ashamed to have their church involved with another scandal on the heels of the nationwide scandal involving priests molesting children.

***

The Baltimore Sun
November 1, 2003

Ex-Worker at Seminary Guilty of Embezzling∗
Frank Langfitt

A former office manager at St. Mary's Seminary & University in Roland Park — who faked her suicide to avoid capture — pleaded guilty yesterday to stealing more than $200,000 from the venerable Catholic institution, according to the State Attorney's office in Baltimore.

Cynthia Jean Downs, 47, continued to be held on $2 million bail at the Baltimore City Detention Center last night. Sentencing is set for Jan. 9.

Under a plea agreement, Downs could receive a maximum sentence of eight years in prison followed by five years of probation. She is also required to pay back the money she stole from St. Mary's, the nation's first Catholic seminary.

When Downs began working at St Mary's in September 1999, the seminary did not know she had served a prison sentence for embezzlement.
*Reprinted with permission of *The Baltimore Sun.*

Commentary: In her final thirteen months, Downs stole more than 90 checks written by clients and deposited them in a dummy account she'd established in the center's name at a local bank. The seminary discovered that money was missing from its bank account during an annual audit and notified the state attorney's office. Downs hid the thefts by paying off some of the institutions oldest,

14

largest outstanding accounts receivable before seminary officials caught onto the scam.

"She was quite expert," the prosecutor noted. "There was a fairly sophisticated scheme she had, to try to keep some of the overdue bills off the books." It was noted in the trial that Downs had a family member who had serious gambling and alcohol problems, and Downs felt she was, in effect, 'coerced into giving money to that person.'"

***

Paralleling the expanded amount of cases, the number of articles in the press increased and significant research was forthcoming. A 2004 article by Tom Feeney (16) in the *Chicago Tribune* drove home a point when he quoted Maria Cleary, Regional Coordinator of the Reform Group, Voice of the Faithful, in the New Jersey dioceses of Paterson, Newark, and Metuchen: "I would guess that there have been many, many more priests that have abused parish finances than ever abused children... The Church has never done enough to stop it." Cleary's telling statement pointed out, *thievery among priests was common knowledge* among those inside the system.

Feeney went on to use the remarks by Edward U. Kmiec, Bishop of the Diocese of Buffalo, to remind readers the "faith-based" doctrine was alive and well, when he said, "It's too expensive and unwieldy for the diocese to conduct annual audits of its parishes."

In another 2004 article, entitled "Embezzlement — It Can Happen to You," Byers and Hurlburt (6) indicated embezzlements occur one out of 20 times in business. A year later, Herbert Lowe (28) reported in *Newsday.com* that in all churches nationwide, the ratio was one in five. Clearly, the trusting environment of churches adds challenges for all church officials.

In late 2004, a theft case by Reverend Joseph W. Hughes ushered in a new era; and one that would propel the thievery scandal forward at an increased rate. The $500,000-plus he stole put him in the upper dollar echelon at the time, but more importantly, his name became a topic of conversation along the East Coast.

Ministering in an upscale town on the Jersey Shore seriously, he took his role of being a part of the community — engaging actively in the country club, eating at the finest restaurants, traveling abroad, and giving gifts to his "personal friend," a young male.

This was the beginning of a series of major cases. Over the next three years, priests would be convicted of thievery to the tune of $1M, $1.3M, $.8M, and $1.3M. While the amount of national attention each received varied considerably, public awareness of the thievery scandal grew.

Reverend Lisowski's scam in Chicago began to collapse when he was caught with a prostitute.

Father Kelly's actions, which took place in the highly populated Cape Cod area, received only spotted recognition beyond the immediate area. Still, more and more people began to hear about financial misconduct.

In New York City, Reverend Woolsey became the first priest in that highly populated center to be convicted of thievery that was not associated with sex offenses.

However, *none of these captured the opulent lifestyle of Father Fay*, who was pictured far and wide from his church in Rumson, New Jersey. The novelty of a priest wearing the finest suits, driving a Jaguar, and staying at the Ritz, was a totally new experience for most.

***

Rumson Priest Stole at Least $500,000 — Upwards of $2 Million Missing*
December 31, 2004

RUMSON, NJ — A crown jewel of the Jersey Shore — known for its quiet wealth and shaded lawns — is the center of an investigation of the Rev. Joseph W. Hughes.

The Catholic Church has been reeling for two years with revelations about clergy sex abuse. But critics say the arrest of Hughes last month, and trials of at least a dozen other priests nationally suggest the church has not done enough to

address another scandal — the theft of parish funds by priests.

In the case of Hughes, he fit right into the community, driving a $57,000 BMW, golfing regularly at the Rumson Country Club, touting his frequent worldwide vacations, and, of course, showing off his big diamond ring. He seemed to dine out every night at pricey restaurants like the Fromagerie or Harry's Lobster Restaurant.

The local Prosecutor's Office announced that, between 2001 and 2004, Hughes allegedly misappropriated at least $500,000 of the church funds to cover personal expenses such as limo rentals and airline tickets and bestow gifts on a 25-year-old male "personal friend."

*Composite article based upon stories reported in the 11/6/04 issue of *Star-Ledger* (NJ), the 12/28/04 issue of *Religion News Services*, and the 12/31/04 issue of the *Chicago Tribune*.

Commentary: This was one of the first, "big-time cases" where a priest was living a flamboyant lifestyle. The rectory and simple white wood-shingled church was set on nearly six rolling acres of prime property and had annual collections of $750,000. Hughes fit in with the community; most people believed he had inherited family money. A few parishioners made a point of his lifestyle but were rebutted — after all, he was *the priest.*

"Certainly, he did not dedicate his life to the lifestyle of a vow of poverty," said the first assistant prosecutor. There were "obvious failures of internal controls" at Holy Cross.

His friend performed maintenance work for his $50,000-a-year contract at Hughes' church. Hughes also bought him jewelry, a giant-screen TV, appliances, a home (for which he paid the mortgage and utility bills) and paid for trips to Bermuda and Cancun.

***

The Morning Call

January 4, 2005

Bookkeeper Stole More than $120,000 from Local Church*

A former bookkeeper at St. Elizabeth of Hungary Catholic Church in Pen Argyl (PA) embezzled more than $121,000 over nearly four years, borough police said.

According to *The Morning Call,* theft, fraud and forgery charges were filed against Jo-Ann Mary Dilullo, who started with the parish as a part-timer in 1991, became the full-time bookkeeper in 2000.

In court papers, police said Dilullo had siphoned parish funds from various accounts since March 2001.
*Reprinted in accordance with "fair use" guidelines.

Commentary: The theft received considerable local attention, since (at the time) it was the largest fraud case in the city's history. As the Church bookkeeper, Dilullo processed all checks for payment and used a signature stamp bearing the priest's name to sign the checks, and wrote numerous unauthorized checks from various accounts, payable to herself. Some checks were never recorded in the Church computer. She created a deposit for the checks received, but not for the cash.

Once again, a trusting environment with no controls, no checks and balances, and no council oversight produced a condition ready for something negative to happen... and it did!

***

Church Stunned by $1.2 Million Theft by Priest*
February 2005

CHICAGO — A letter from the bishop read at mass sent shockwaves through members of the St. Bede the Venerable

Church. He had been caught with a suspected prostitute last summer, and Reverend Brian Lisowski had misappropriated $1,144,380.

Lisowski resigned last July.

The theft became apparent when the amount gathered in collections increased dramatically after that — the system caught up with Lisowski, Archdiocese spokesman Jim Dwyer said.

Over five years, Lisowski made regular trips to the bank, depositing nearly $450,000 in checking and money market accounts. Prosecutors said one person, whom they described as a "close female friend," received $262,000 from Lisowski.

Prosecutors noted he'd tried to cover his tracks by making false entries in the church's accounting books. After admitting to the theft, Lisowski led church officials to a safe-deposit box containing nearly $400,000 and a safe in his bedroom with over $50,000 in cash and $600 in coins.

*Composite article based upon stories reported in the 9/12/04 issue of the *Chicago Tribune,* the 9/13/04 issue of *nwitimes.com.,* and the 2/12/05 issue of *The Washington Post.*

Commentary: "Most cases of church embezzlement go unreported," said the prosecutor, "congregations often are embarrassed by what has happened and are unwilling to go to the police. The biggest issue in a case like this is the violation of trust… It's not about the money so much. It's about trust."

The priest established separate accounts, which gave him what an embezzler needs to succeed — access without accountability — he could transfer funds without the knowledge of anyone else.

***

Cape Cod Times

April 4, 2006

Father Kelly's House Faces Foreclosure*

BARNSTABLE — The *Cape Cod Times* reports, a Barnstable Superior Court judge authorized the Fall River Diocese to foreclose on an embattled priest's Cummaquid estate yesterday.

Retired Catholic Priest Bernard Kelly agreed to pay the diocese $1.3 million for funds he misspent as pastor at two Cape Cod parishes, according to the *Times*. Kelly faced scrutiny from the diocese in October 2003, when police investigators wanted to question him about the death of Jonathan Wesser, 20, of Falmouth, who was murdered by Paul Nolan.

Nolan, who allegedly had a sexual relationship with Kelly, visited the priest frequently in the days after the murder, says the *Times*. Nolan is now serving a life sentence.

*Reprinted in accordance with "fair use" guidelines.

Commentary: Typical of the times, while this became a public matter, the issue was settled for the most part between the Church and Father Kelly. It's noteworthy to point out that Kelly's estate was listed for $3.5M. While he was facing criminal charges for embezzlement and not filing tax returns, the price dropped to $2.1M, and the property was listed as a bed and breakfast.

***

Msgr. Moneybags — Loaded with Cash and Stock*

September 22, 2006

4-Year Prison Term for Priest Accused of Stealing from Parish

A pillar of the Roman Catholic church in New York suffered an extraordinary fall today as a judge sentenced Monsignor John G. Woolsey to four years in prison. He was accused of stealing more than $800,000 from his former church, St. John the Martyr, in the affluent Upper East Side.

He had a lifestyle more in keeping with that of a corporate chief executive, including golf outings, the purchase of expensive watches, and cosmetic dental work. Investigators from the Manhattan District Attorney's office discovered how the charismatic priest funded his posh lifestyle, which included an account at Brooks Brothers, showy Rolex watches, and luxury cars.

Justice Allen said he had been touched by the more than 140 "letters from the heart," delivered to him from Monsignor Woolsey's friends, fellow priests, and parishioners. As a result, he reduced the priest sentence by a year, then sentenced him to one to four years in prison and to pay $50,000 in addition to the $200,000 that the Monsignor had already paid.

Standing in for the ousted Msgr. Woolsey, the associate pastor tried to set a new tone by providing a play-by-play accounting of the parish's financial transactions. "These are the accounts," the Rev. Joseph Baker said, holding up bank statements from the church's checking and saving accounts. "This is your parish, you make it up; not the priests, we're just the employees."

"I'm not hiding anything from you — it's not my money. It's your money," Baker said to reporters after Mass. "You should never be afraid of the truth."

*Composite article based upon stories reported in the 7/19/04 issue of the *Cult Education Institute,* the 8/12/04 issue of the *New York Post,* and the 9/22/06 issue of the *New York Times.*

Commentary: This case is particularly noteworthy because it represents the first priest to be convicted of financial crimes, not associated with sex offenses, in at least two decades in the highly populated archdiocese, which included Manhattan, the Bronx, Staten Island, and seven suburban counties.

Woolsey had abused the trust of parishioners by telling them he was spending their donations on repairs to the church when he was spending their money on his own lavish lifestyle. Monsignor Woolsey said his parishioners wanted him to be able to use some of their money for himself.

***

Catholic World News
August 5, 2009 (Case uncovered in 2006)

Lawsuit, Deposition Allege Diocese Played Hardball with Whistleblower Priest, Accountant*

A lawsuit filed by Bethany D'Erario, a former parish accountant, alleges that the Diocese of Bridgeport created a hostile work environment after she and an assistant priest, Father Michael Madden, hired a private investigator to examine the suspicious financial dealings of the parish's pastor, Father Michael Jude Fay.

After the private investigator turned over information to police, Father Fay was arrested and eventually sentenced to prison for embezzling $1 million.

Fay, who pleaded guilty to a federal fraud charge in September, set up secret bank accounts to pay for travel around the world and to buy a condominium.

The former priest who stole about $1.3 million from his parish to support a life of luxury was sentenced Tuesday to 37 months in prison. The Rev. Michael Jude Fay also was ordered to pay $1 million in restitution.

Ms. D'Erario also alleged that Father Fay had a homosexual affair with a finance council member.

In a deposition given in connection with the lawsuit, Madden — who sought to leave the priesthood in 2006 — alleges that Bishop William Lori threatened to send him to a nuns' convent in retaliation after he found out he hired a private investigator. The diocesan attorney responded that "at no time did Bishop Lori ever threaten to send Mr. Madden to live with nuns."

In an extremely aggressive public response to the lawsuit, the Bridgeport diocese told Catholic News Agency that all the charges brought by Madden and D'Erario are untrue, and that their lawsuit is an effort to "use inflammatory rhetoric as a substitute for evidence." The diocese further charged that in filing suit D'Erario's motives were "financial rather than any real claim of wrongdoing or injustice." The diocese suggested that D'Erario hired a private investigator to probe Father Fay's financial affairs only to protect herself from accusations of wrongdoing; and noted that it was the diocese that finally brought the financial misconduct to the attention of local prosecutors.

*Reprinted with permission from *Catholic World News*.

Commentary: This was the most notorious thievery case to appear in the early years. Reverend Fay's personal actions gave him "celebrity-like" status. The case reads like a soap-opera — he had secret bank accounts to pay for travel around the world, drove a Jaguar around the east coast, and stayed in world-class hotels.

When using church funds, Fay went first-class in every venture — he spent $130,000 on limousines and had stayed at the Ritz Carlton, Hotel De Paris, and the Four Seasons Hotel. He purchased jewelry from Cartier, shopped at Bergdorf Goodman, Saks Fifth Avenue, and Nordstrom.

In court, Fay made an analogy to Leonardo da Vinci's painting of The Last Supper, citing a story that the same man who stood in as a model for Judas cried out that, years earlier, he was the model for John. "I stand before you a canvas of multiple layers," he declared.

"Day of great sorrow," U.S. District Judge Janet Bond Arterton said, and that Fay's actions were carried out over several years and ultimately devastated church members. "The sentence," she said, "is a message that not even the collar can protect you from prison."

***

Chicago Priest Steals $200,000 for Male Stripper*
November 29, 2007

The Reverend Mark Sorvillo dined at expensive restaurants and shopped at luxury stores. It took a sting to prove he was stealing.

CHICAGO, IL — Reverend Mark Sorvillo pleaded guilty of stealing St. Margaret Mary parish funds for his own use. While he enjoyed the good life, the Reverend spent most of the money on a married gay-for-pay male stripper.

The state attorney's office charged him with stealing nearly $200,000 from his parish to support a lavish lifestyle of travel, attendance at Lyric Opera, and shopping at luxury department stores.

"This was an eight-year pattern of continuing deceit and greed," the prosecutor said. "The defendant took full advantage of his parishioners' understandable reluctance to vigorously question his actions."

Another disconcerting aspect of the story is when the parish business manager warned the chancery of Sorvillo's questionable spending habits, he was told to "keep his yap shut" and then was fired. The business manager was not charged with any wrongdoing.
*Composite article based upon stories reported in the 6/14/2007 issue of the *Chicago Sun-Times,* the 11/26/07 issue *Commonweal Magazine,* and the 11/29/07 issue of the *Chicago Magazine.*

Commentary: The parishioners caught Sorvillo through both a rebellion against his decision to close the school and a sting operation that proved he was stealing funds. In addition to funds used for himself, as cited above, he gave the stripper $1000 a month and bought him clothing, a Dell computer, a motorcycle, and a car for the stripper's wife.

"It's been a long and emotional road," said Dan McGuire, one of three parishioners who led an internal audit that revealed Sorvillo's financial extravagances.

***

In a landmark study, entitled "Internal Financial Controls in the U. S. Catholic Church," by Robert West and Charles Zech (51), they found 85 percent of the dioceses in the nation had experienced embezzlements during the previous five years.

The following percentages may not seem significant at first glance, but if the number of parishes in the country were evenly distributed over the 197 dioceses (19,000 parishes at the time), it would mean:

- 3 percent of the dioceses, nationwide, annually conducted an internal audit of the parishes (97 percent failed to do so, suggests over 18,000 parishes could have been at risk).

- 21 percent of the dioceses seldom or never audited their parishes (21 percent suggests up to 4000 could have not been audited).

- 29 percent of the dioceses, nationwide, reported thefts of less than $50,000 (29 percent suggests as many as 5500 parishes could have had thefts).

- 11 percent of the dioceses reported embezzlements of more than $500,000 (11 percent suggests over 2000 parishes could have had major embezzlements).

"We're too trusting," said Charles Zech, former head of the Center for the Study of Church Management and Business Ethics at Villanova University. "No one would expect a priest or minister to embezzle or a church worker to embezzle."

The findings in this prominent research provided the bishops with plenty of fuel to take aggressive corrective action.

CHAPTER THREE
Thievery Scandal Flows
2008

The amplified attention given to thievery as a result of the research by West and Zech in 2007 seemed to produce an increased number of articles focused on the topic. Likewise, acting through their Diocesan Fiscal Management Council (14), the USCCB produced its strongest language to date, *requiring all dioceses* to conduct yearly internal audits of their parishes — with the pastor, key employees, and finance council members signing-off on the documents, attesting:

> ... They have not received any report that has not been reported to the diocesan bishop... of fraud, abuse, or misappropriation, and that the signers have not engaged in any activity with the priest from which they have, or their family could personally benefit.

Dioceses across the country made new statements of ethical action, illustrated by the statement from the Diocese of St. Petersburg (Florida), dated July 1, 2008:

> In the ministries of parishes and schools, we are the stewards of the goods of the Church. Our Church and its beliefs are of the highest value, inspired by God. Therefore, our actions must always emulate the sanctity of the Church and be modeled to achieve the trust of the Christian-faithful. As such, pastors and principals are required to develop and implement Standards of Ethical Behavior and Professional Conduct that inspire all of the personnel of your parishes

and schools to live those values in the daily conduct of the business and management of the ministry.

Once again, the thievery cases in 2008 and the following years indicated the action taken by the USCCB was little more than window dressing. Those parishes that followed proper procedures continued to do so, taking actions, as directed. And those who ignored the directives in the past continued to do so, without retribution.

Jay Tokasz (44) illustrated the point with the number of white-collar thefts in the Church. Erie County (NY) alone cost the Catholic parishes and schools a combined $1.7M. He concluded parish pilfering wasn't limited to Western New York by stressing, "Leaders across the country are wrestling with how to prevent what once was thought of as an unthinkable crime."

Quoting the local district attorney, Tokasz noted, "'Certainly the dollars have increased geometrically... I used to see thefts of $14,000 to $16,000; lately they have ranged from $230,000 to $488,000.'"

In another 2008 story, Tokasz referred to the *Chicago Tribune* report of Catholic priest, Steven Patte, caught stealing from the offering plate. A Chicago police detective, who was on the parish finance committee, became suspicious about accounting discrepancies and placed a marked $100 bill in the collection plate.

Patte pleaded guilty to stealing $12,000 and was reassigned to another church. After his reassignment, officials discovered the surplus at the church was gone and their church was $400,000 in debt.

Thievery of this type (43) is referred to as skimming — slang for a form of white-collar crime, for taking cash "off the top" and officially reporting a lower total. The formal legal term is defalcation.

For the first time, in the same year, a broad array of devious strategies appeared, including an elaborate kickback scheme by a chief financial officer, an embezzlement by a bookkeeper, and several outright thefts by priests, deacons, and secretaries. At the heart of these cases was the "faith-based" philosophy; individuals throughout a system with an inconsistent use of checks and balances are *simply too trusting.*

Thievery as measured by notable cases also took a small step upward in 2008, reaching $2,645,000. More importantly, the number of cases over $100,000 more than doubled the number of cases reported in 2007.

The increased number of cases turned out to be a significant development. An increased number of news stories began to appear in small-town weeklies, city dailies, and urban mega-media outlets.

***

The growing volume of stories in chapters 3 through 13 focus on a single year. In each chapter, a chart depicting the total amount of dollars of cases over $100,000 for that year and the five previous years are illustrated.

Chart 3, which follows, illustrates this approach.

The five white columns on the left represent the previous five years. The black column on the right adds the data for 2008. In succeeding chapters, a new black column is added on the right for that year and the first white column on the left is dropped off.

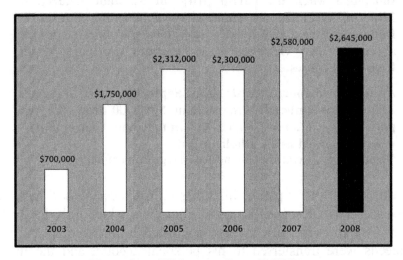

Chart 3 — Thievery Scandal Flows

gmanetwork.com

February 22, 2008

RP Priest Gets Five-year Jail Term in US for Embezzlement*

By Joseph G. Lariosa

CHICAGO, IL — Filipino priest, Rev. Rodney L. Rodis was sentenced Thursday, Feb. 21 to one count of mail fraud and one count of money laundering to 63 months each in federal prison and was ordered to pay full restitution to the Catholic Diocese of Virginia in the amount of $491,484.08.

Rodis, 51, of Fredericksburg, Virginia, and believed to have hailed from Cagayan de Oro City in the Philippines, will be serving more than five years of prison terms concurrently and will be credited for time served, according to Laura Taylor, public information officer of the United States Attorney for the Eastern District of Virginia in Richmond.

It took United States District Judge Richard L. Williams only 27 minutes to deliver the sentence in open court. Williams also placed Rodis under supervised release for three years.

The sentence ended year-long court litigation that was shortened when the parish priest of St. Jude Church in Mineral, Virginia, and Immaculate Conception Church of Bumpass, Virginia, waived a jury trial and entered a plea agreement last October. Both churches are part of the Richmond Diocese.

According to court records, from September 2002 to August 2006, Rodis embezzled more than $600,000 from the two parishes — St. Jude Church and Immaculate Conception — where he served as a Catholic priest.

*Reprinted with permission from Mediamerge Corporation.

Commentary: As part of his scheme, Rodis established his own bank accounts and opened a post office box, which only he could open. Church contributions were deposited in his account and the proceeds were transferred to his personal account and the funds were then wired to his family in the Philippines.

The embezzled funds were used by his family members to purchase property including beachfront locations. Court records show that Rodis was leading a double life as a family man in the Philippines with a wife and two biological children.

***

Newspapergroup.com
Manalapan Archives
April 4, 2008

Ex-church Bookkeeper Gets Five Years for Payroll Theft*
By Karen Bowes

FREEHOLD, NJ — A woman who admitted stealing over $800,000 from St. Benedict's Roman Catholic Church, Holmdel, was sentenced to five years in prison on Friday. As part of her sentence, she must also pay back the money.

Joan Orlando, 61, Toms River, pleaded guilty on Jan. 22 to theft by deception, a second-degree crime, and failure to pay New Jersey state income taxes, a third-degree crime.

Orlando's husband, Richard Orlando, 61, was also indicted in connection with the theft. He is pending trial, scheduled for May 21.

Orlando was employed as the bookkeeper and finance administrator of St. Benedict's beginning in 1998. In her position, she had sole responsibility for, among other things, parish payroll. According to the Monmouth County Prosecutor's Office, Orlando admitted that between 2001 and June of 2005, she submitted inflated salary figures for herself to the payroll processing company. As part of the scheme, Orlando received over $800,000 in excess salary. To conceal the theft, she altered tax records.

On Monday, Rayanne Bennett, a spokesperson for the Diocese of Trenton, talked about the importance of remembering the fundamentals of Christianity about this matter.

"We keep her and her family in our prayers because this is obviously a difficult time," Bennett said.

Superior Court Judge Paul F. Chaiet ordered Orlando to pay $25,000 in restitution to St. Benedict's over a five-year period. Orlando also agreed to a civil judgment requiring her to pay back $588,163 to Travelers Insurance Co., and $245,793.11 to St. Benedict's.

*Reprinted with permission of newspapergroup.com.

Commentary: Once again, this case illustrates the problem of a faith-based organization having one person, with no checks and balances, in control of the finances. When asked if the parish and school have suffered as a result of the theft, the spokesperson for the diocese noted that much of the money has already been returned through the insurance company.

Sounding like nothing had ever happened, she said, "The parish is doing very well under the pastorship of the newly appointed Father Dan Swift... The sentencing gives needed closure to the parish."

***

Journal Sentinel
July 2008

Former Church Bookkeeper Sentenced in Theft Case*

WAUKESHA, WI — The *Journal Sentinel* reports, a former church bookkeeper paid back a portion of the money she is convicted of stealing from her Menomonee Falls parish before being sentenced Thursday to 30 days in jail and 18 months of probation.

Janet E. Pachmayer, 56, of Mequon was convicted of three misdemeanor theft charges. She faces about two years in prison, according to the *Journal Sentinel.*

Pachmayer paid $79,000 in restitution. An audit showed she took an estimated $134,000 while employed at St. Anthony Catholic Church.

Pachmayer, who worked at the church from 2002 to 2008, had told investigators that she stole from the church to support her children after a divorce.

She had been charged with felony theft and faced up to 10 years in prison, if convicted, court records show. In a plea agreement, the charges were downgraded to three misdemeanor theft charges in exchange for Pachmayer's guilty plea and payment of restitution.

Conditions of her probation include payment of $294 in fines and attendance at any treatment her probation agent deems necessary, the *Journal Sentinel* said. She is prohibited from contacting the church and from gaining employment in which she'll be in charge of finances.
*Reprinted in accordance with "fair use" guidelines.

Commentary: One more time, the trickle-down effect of the "faith-based" doctrine left a woman who was improperly supervised, who had a "need" to support her family, with the "opportunity" to commit a crime.

***

Department of Justice
IMMEDIATE RELEASE
December 11, 2008

Former Chief Financial Officer of Catholic Diocese of Cleveland Sentenced to a Year and a Day in Prison for Tax Crimes*

WASHINGTON - Joseph H. Smith, a CPA and attorney, was sentenced today to a year and a day in prison by U.S. District Judge Ann Aldrich for his participation in a scheme to defraud the Internal Revenue Service (IRS). Following a six-week trial, a jury in Cleveland convicted Smith of one count of conspiracy to defraud the United States and IRS, four counts of filing false tax returns, and one count of corruptly endeavoring to impede the IRS.

Smith was the treasurer, chief financial officer, and eventually the financial and legal secretary for the Catholic Diocese of Cleveland. Co-conspirator Anton Zgoznik, a former diocese employee, owned and operated several corporations that provided accounting, tax, financial, and computer technology services for the diocese on an outsourced basis.

During the trial, it was shown that Smith and Zgoznik entered into a scheme to defraud the IRS. Entities that Zgoznik owned and controlled paid Smith more than $784,000 from 1997 to 2003. Smith and Zgoznik disguised these payments as compensation earned for "consulting" or "legal" services that Smith purportedly provided to the Zgoznik entities.

*Reprinted from public news release.

Commentary: This highly complex case led to a series of convictions. In a separate trial, Zgoznik was convicted on 15 counts of conspiracy to commit mail fraud and four counts of aiding and assisting in the preparation of a false return. As a result of their scheme, they deceived the IRS on their tax returns for three years. Both men were also convicted on numerous counts for an elaborate kickback scheme.

Smith was the highest-ranking layperson of the diocese, serving as chief financial officer. Prosecutors accused him of approving inflated billings from Zgoznik, who in turn paid money to companies owned by Smith.

The scheme was uncovered when a whistle-blower sent an anonymous letter to the diocese outlining the payments to Smith and Zgoznik.

Retired Bishop Anthony Pilla of Cleveland said he was, "Shocked. I had complete trust in Mr. Smith. He was a valued co-worker in whom I had great trust."

CHAPTER FOUR
Passed Over Thievery
2009

In sharp contrast to Church rhetoric, Paul Gorrell (20), a former Catholic priest, pointed out the thievery scandal had been passed over. In a scathing article in "Religious Dispatches," he indicated the amount of thievery in the Church is the result of a "potentially larger and more pervasive problem within the Catholic hierarchy that may reflect a moral collapse that is decades old."

Some of his salient points include the following:

> Within the last decade, the Catholic Church has begun to grapple with a crisis that turns out to be more pervasive than first imagined. Catholics and the press are beginning to connect the dots, just as they did in the sexual abuse crisis, and are spotting a larger pattern.

> I would argue that a scandal of this magnitude creates a new round of questions about the current model of the priesthood.

> Based on medieval definitions of the role of a bishop, Catholic pastors have both custodial and visionary responsibilities within their assigned parish. Protestants typically separate these responsibilities, with the laity having oversight of the finances, allowing their clergy full devotion to ministerial duties.

> Individual stories of embezzlement point to a potentially larger and more pervasive problem within the Catholic hierarchy that may reflect a moral collapse that is decades old — although, unlike the pedophilia scandal, there are no

individual victims in these situations to come forward and expose latent crimes. We may never know the true extent of this problem in the Catholic Church.

Gorrell concluded his article by saying:

> The latest discovery of thefts by priests is yet another reason to examine the theology and polity of the Roman Catholic priesthood. While individual scandals grab the headlines, it is important to examine the patterns and shine the clear light of day on the systemic problems within the Roman Catholic priesthood.

***

From small cases to large attention-getters, Gorrell's comments appear to be on target and to the point; but the Bishops' actions back in 2007 to introduce more stringent requirements to prevent thievery had no effect — thievery cases in 2008 and again in 2009 continued to grow across-the-board.

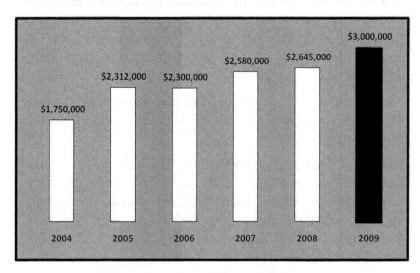

Chart 4 — Passed Over Thievery

As illustrated in chart 4, the dollar impact of notable cases hit $3M, up over $350,000 from 2008, and still no one seemed to pay attention. The highlight for the year occurred in Florida. Two priests skimmed money from collection plates and bequests made to their church in Delray Beach, Florida. Forensic accountants hired by the diocese found that $8.7M had been misappropriated from the St. Vincent Ferrer Church during the tenures of Skehan and his successor, Guinan. Records show they spent hundreds of thousands of dollars on real estate, travel, rare coins, and girlfriends.

***

Sun Sentinel
March 25, 2009

Priest Who Stole Gets 14 Months in Prison*
Andy Reid

Old age and the support of the Catholic Church couldn't spare a disgraced former pastor from prison time for stealing from his Delray Beach congregation.

The Rev. John Skehan, 81, was sentenced to 14 months in prison Tuesday for grand theft of more than $100,000 from St. Vincent Ferrer Catholic Church. He must surrender to begin serving the term by May 1.

Investigators say Skehan stole $370,000 that he spent on a girlfriend, trips, homes, and other property in Florida and his native Ireland.

Palm Beach Circuit Judge Jeffrey Colbath cited Skehan's "sincere contrition" and advanced age for imposing a lesser sentence. But he said Skehan violated the "sacred trust of loyal and faithful parishioners" and should be incarcerated.

"The crime of the defendant was pure greed unmasked," Colbath said at the sentencing. "There was not a shred of moral necessity to excuse the defendant's crime."

Skehan had faced between 22 months and 30 years in prison for his crimes. He pleaded guilty in January, avoiding a trial. He entered an "open plea," meaning he threw himself on the mercy of the judge, and there were no guarantees of what sentence he would receive.

Colbath also sentenced Skehan to seven years of probation, and Skehan is forbidden to return to St. Vincent or participate in church activities there.

The Diocese of Palm Beach and a parade of supporters, including priests and parishioners, had urged leniency for Skehan. The diocese asked for restitution, not jail time, and Colbath delayed making a decision until Friday.

Skehan told the judge Friday that he was ashamed and sorry.

"The simple truth is, deep in my heart, I thought I was doing the right thing," Skehan said. "For over 50 years, I saw my role as priest caring for people . . . helping them spiritually, emotionally and assisting them financially when I saw they needed it."

Skehan said the pain he feels will never go away.

"It's a disappointment, but Father Skehan is a man of faith and he will persevere," defense attorney Scott Richardson said. "He has been remorseful from the very beginning."

Skehan surrendered a condominium worth $366,000 as restitution, as well as $39,000 in cash and a coin collection estimated to be worth about $381,000.

"Giving back the money once he got caught and serving probation alone would not have been enough punishment," said retired Delray Beach police Detective Tom Whatley, who investigated the case against Skehan.

"It would have sent the message, 'Hey, it's OK to take money... You might get off,'" said Whatley, who was in court.

*Reprinted with permission of the *Sun Sentinel.*

Commentary: Skehan, 81, was sentenced to 14 months in prison and seven years of probation. When the priests were charged in September 2006, police said they had channeled money from collection plates into secret slush funds, using some of it for church projects and part for purchasing property, taking vacations, and gambling trips to Las Vegas and the Bahamas.

Investigators said Skehan, a priest for more than 50 years, invested heavily in rare coins, owned a cottage and a pub in Ireland, a

$455,000 penthouse condominium on Singer Island, Florida, and another apartment in Delray Beach.

***

Judge Sentences Second Delray Beach Priest to 4 years in Prison*
March 29, 2009

MIAMI – A second Roman Catholic priest, Rev. Francis Guinan, was sentenced to prison in a case involving the misappropriation of more than $8 million from his Delray Beach church. He was found guilty of a charge of theft under $100,000.

Guinan stole the money from 2003 to 2005 to take trips to Ireland and Las Vegas, dine at expensive restaurants, and pay personal credit card expenses.

Guinan told a jury he could spend his Delray Beach church's money however he wanted, on trips to Las Vegas, expensive dinners and golf outings. He pointed out that it was normal to lie in church bank records, create secret slush funds, and walk away from the offertory with wads of cash.

Palm Beach Circuit Judge Krista Marx had one word for those claims: "Malarkey... These excuses, the myriad excuses, it's malarkey. You are in this situation because of your unmitigated greed and unmitigated gall."

The Diocese of Palm Beach County has banned both men from ministering to the public, though they remain priests.
*Composite article based upon stories reported in the 3/27/09 issue of the *Miami Herald,* the 11/26/07 issue *Commonweal Magazine,* and the 11/29/07 issue of the *Chicago Magazine.*

Commentary: According to the charges, Rev. Francis Guinan, another Irish priest, and Skehan operated, in what authorities say could be one of the biggest embezzlement cases to hit the US Catholic Church.

The trial of Guinan, who has pleaded not guilty, has been delayed. He was accused of stealing $488,000 over 19 months after he became the pastor in September 2003.

Authorities, also, alleged Guinan had an "intimate relationship" with a former bookkeeper at a church where he had previously worked, which included paying her credit card bills and her child's school tuition with money that was not recorded on the Church books. They said the woman accompanied the priest on holidays.

***

The Journal News
October 20, 2009

White Plains Ex-Pastor Pleads Guilty to Stealing $432,000*

WHITE PLAINS, CT — Had the Rev. Patrick Dunne been convicted after trial for stealing $432,000 from his White Plains church, he could have been sent to state prison for 15 years, *The Journal News* says; instead, he was convicted through a plea bargain and won't serve any more than six months in the county jail.

According to *The Journal News,* Dunne, the 63-year-old former pastor of Our Lady of Sorrows Church, pleaded guilty today to the top count against him, second-degree grand larceny, a felony, in Westchester County Court in exchange for "shock" probation, in which he will serve five years' probation with some time in jail.

Dunne, who led the Mamaroneck Avenue church since 1991, stole the money over a six-year period — including donations intended for Hurricane Katrina victims — and used it for personal expenses and recreation, including gambling, *The Journal News* reported.

And, *The Journal News* indicated, as part of the plea deal, Dunne must pay restitution to the Roman Catholic Archdiocese of New York up to $432,000.

Dunne's attorney, Richard Ferrante, would not say how his client planned to repay the archdiocese. He said Dunne has completed an inpatient treatment program for his gambling addiction and is undergoing outpatient treatment.
*Reprinted in accordance with "fair use' guidelines.

Commentary: The stolen money had been donated by parishioners to different fundraising efforts by the Church, such as the building fund, a collection for Katrina victims, and weekly offering used for general church expenses. Money was also taken from an account that had been set up to pay clergy members who came to the Church to celebrate Mass.

The case appeared before a grand jury in May after months of negotiations failed to produce a plea bargain. Prosecutors had lobbied for Dunne to serve state prison time but agreeing to a jail sentence instead. The archdiocese's insurance company covered the Church's loss.

***

St. Louis Post-Dispatch
November 24, 2009

Man Admits Embezzling $510,000 from School Sisters of Notre Dame*

The *Post-Dispatch* reported that the former head of information technology for the St. Louis Province of the School Sisters of Notre Dame, on November 24, 2009, admitted embezzling $510,000, according to the U.S. Attorney's office.

From 2000 through 2007, Paul Steven Murphy submitted fake invoices from a company that he had created and hid his ownership of the company from other employees, his plea agreement says.

Murphy used the money for jewelry, mortgage payments, restaurants, and trips to Hawaii, Las Vegas, and India, prosecutors said.

Murphy, 44, pleaded guilty in U.S. District Court in St. Louis to one count of mail fraud and one count of filing false tax returns. Murphy failed to report $112,330 of the embezzled money as income from 2003 to 2007, prosecutors said.

Under federal sentencing guidelines, the *Post-Dispatch* indicated, Murphy faces roughly three to four years in prison when sentenced in February.

*Reprinted in accordance with "fair use" guidelines.

Commentary: Although Murphy's salary nearly doubled from $33,000 in 2003 to $60,000 in 2007, his embezzlement continued unabated. He stole between $55,000 and $106,000 per year, spending $47,000 on travel and entertainment, $35,000 on house payments, and $21,000 on his wedding. Sister Lynne Schmidt said, now there is less money to serve the "poor and dispossessed."

***

The number of cases below $100,000 continued to grow, from coast to coast. In Alaska, a part-time employee at St. Andrews Catholic Church in Eagle River redirected over $27,000 from the direct deposit payroll system to her personal account. She also created false invoices for nearly $10,000 worth of landscaping materials, for which she was charged with scheming to defraud, theft in the first degree, and falsifying business records.

A trusted employee with the East Baton Rouge Parish School System was arrested on December 8, 2009 after allegedly padding her own bank account through private information from fellow workers. Authorities said she used her job as a payroll worker to gain access to part-time employee bank account information.

In Chicago, Reverend John Regan was accused of creating a separate bank account and funneling parish money into it for his own use. Using the money for his gambling activities, he was charged with money laundering.

Two cases in Michigan and one in Ohio were reported within weeks of each other. On December 17, a volunteer bookkeeper at Our Lady Star of the Sea Catholic Church in Grosse Pointe Woods, Michigan pleaded guilty to embezzling more than $90,000. Two days later, police arrested a woman in Greenfield, Ohio on charges of grand theft for stealing more than $40,000 from St. Benignus Catholic Church where she had worked as a secretary for five years. On December 24, a volunteer at St. Vincent de Paul Parish in Pontiac, Michigan was accused of stealing thousands of dollars. In each of these cases, the "trusted" individual had full access to the funds with no checks or balances.

CHAPTER FIVE
The Calm Before the Storm
2010

Venture and Daniel (46), in describing the findings of their research in a 2010 article in the *Journal of Forensic Investigating Accounting*, provided additional insights into why little change occurred after the USBBC strengthened requirements for bishops and priests. They found that 73 percent of parishioners believed Catholic Church leaders possessed the "highest level of honesty" on their scale. Most of the others in the research checked the next category — "high level of honesty." Correspondingly, the participants in the study expressed a low level of need to see the parish's financial records.

Having a high degree of confidence in their leader's ethical behavior, it was easy for parishioners to take the action by the USBBC lightly, with a general attitude like, "Reverend X would never think of stealing, it would never happen here." Obviously, for *the priest* who was not trustworthy, it was easy for him to proverbially "pull the wool over their eyes."

Venture and Daniel illustrated this point, noting that only 54 percent of the parishioners on financial committees said they received annual financial statements. And when they were provided such reports, they gave them little attention.

Not only did their high level of confidence in the leaders reduce a need to see financial disclosures, it also meant that people with *financial oversight expertise were rarely appointed* to the boards. Again, the research verified ongoing practices in many parishes, in which it was common for an individual to say, "I don't see the need for expert advice. I have confidence in how the parish is managed. I don't need to ask about how funds are used."

While statements like these were often made, they are the very reason checks and balances are needed. "Faith-based" organizations depend upon trustworthiness of this type, not everyone is trustworthy.

***

The notable cases for 2010 illustrate the disconnect between approved church policy and actual practice at the parish level. Although notable cases dipped slightly, once again, another major case highlighted the year.

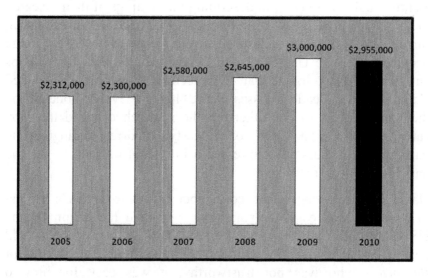

Chart 5 — Calm Before the Storm

***

Priest Steals $1.3 Million for Hotels, Male Escorts*
July 6, 2010

> *Priest said, "he had grown to hate being a priest" because the Archdiocese had given him the "worst church assignments" where he would "have to fix problems made by the previous priests."*

The Rev. Kevin J. Gray, 64, was charged with first-degree larceny for using church funds to pay for hotels, restaurant meals, clothing, and male escorts. Gray was arraigned in Waterbury Superior Court. Bail was set at $750,000, court officials said.

"To his congregation, he lived the humble existence, but when he was out of town, he was a high-flying Connecticut priest. He stole almost $1.3 million from church coffers to fund a lavish double life," said Capt. Chris Corbett of the Waterbury Police Department in Connecticut.

According to an affidavit obtained by CNN affiliate WTIC and filed with the Connecticut Superior Court, the former pastor allegedly embezzled money from the church over the course of seven years. The money was used to pay for fancy restaurants, clothing, vacations, regular hotel stays at the Waldorf Astoria, Omni Berkshire, and the W Hotel Times Square, among other posh hotels, a New York City apartment, and a male companion's tuition at Harvard University.

Waterbury police launched an investigation after the Archdiocese came to them May 27 and said it had uncovered unauthorized payments from church funds to accounts held by Gray and other suspicious transactions, according to the affidavit.

Gray told police he first became bitter when the Archdiocese transferred him to Immaculate Conception Church in New Hartford in 2001 while his mother was dying in a New Haven hospital. He said he was angry that he had to commute too far a few times a week to see his mother.

He was then transferred to St. Cecelia's Church in Waterbury, which closed while he was there. He called the closing a "sham."

Gray told police he was gay and had a problem with the Church's stance on homosexuality.

*Composite article based upon the stories of 7/6/10 issue of the *Harford Courant,* the 7/7/10 issue of *The New Post,* and reported on by CNN on 7/8/10.

Commentary: Some points of special interest in this case are:

- Gray transferred over $655,000 worth of checks from the Church funds to his account to pay American Express charges.

- He charged over $200,000 to restaurants in New York, Boston, and Connecticut, including several visits to New York's Tavern on The Green, Boston's Legal Seafood, and New Haven's Scoozzi Trattoria and Wine Bar.

- Gray charged nearly $150,000 in overnight stays at high-end hotels.

- Gray opened credit card accounts in the names of Manuel Paque, a man he met at a male strip bar, and Islagar Labrada, a man he'd met through an escort service.

- Gray purchased $80,000-plus at clothing stores such as Brooks Brothers, Barney's, and Armani and roughly $20,000 at jewelry stores, including Tiffany's.

- Each parish was to have a financial council to work with the pastor on fiscal matters, but his parishes did not have such a panel. Pastors are also required to issue annual financial reports to the archdiocese. Gray did not comply.

***

Pierce County Herald
February 16, 2010

Priest Charged with Embezzlement in Crawford County*

PRAIRIE DU CHIEN, WI – According to the *Pierce County Herald*, a Catholic priest in southwest Wisconsin stood mute yesterday while a not guilty plea was entered on his felony embezzlement charge.

The 59-year-old Reverend Robert Chukwu is accused of stealing $200,000 from the La Crosse Diocese and the parishes

in Gays Mills and Soldiers Grove. His case is being heard in Crawford County, the *County Herald* reported.

Prosecutors said Chukwu gave cash to a nun, priests, a family, and a school in Nigeria from 2007 through last year. And he allegedly sent a 40-foot container to Nigeria with one hundred thousand dollars' worth of candlesticks, artificial flowers, and a lot more. Chukwu has dual citizenship in Nigeria and the U.S. authorities said. Chukwu bought the merchandise on a debit card with insurance money from the heavy floods in southwest Wisconsin in 2007.

*Reprinted in accordance with "fair use" guidelines.

Commentary: Chukwu used the money from the 2007 flood damage to facilitate his scam. He charged the parishes' debit cards with $200,000 worth of items minus any invoices — about $100,000 for which he was reimbursed. When objection was raised about some of his practices, he disbanded the finance council.

The diocese ultimately noticed an excessive amount of long-distance charges and hired an independent accounting firm to review parish books.

✳✳✳

Lowellsun.com
June 1, 2010

Ex-Tyngsboro Church Worker Indicted on Embezzlement Charges*

LOWELL, MA — A former Tyngsboro church employee has been indicted for allegedly skimming well over $100,000 from the cash donations made by the parishioners at Sunday Masses, including donations made to the poor, at St. Mary Magdalen Parish.

Donna Rood, 47, of Tyngsboro, has been indicted on charges of larceny by embezzlement over $250 and making false entries in corporate books.

"This defendant is alleged to have violated the trust and faith bestowed upon her as an employee of this church by stealing the monetary donations that were intended for the needs of her church and community," Middlesex District Attorney Gerard Leone said in a statement. "We allege that the defendant sadly abused this trust stealing well over $100,000 from charitable collection baskets during her time of employment."

According to authorities, Rood had access to the cash and books at the Tyngsboro church from 2003 until June of 2009. One of her responsibilities in the parish was to count charitable donations made by the parishioners during the three Sunday Masses. Donations were made by both check and cash, and included donations to the building fund, which served to maintain the church grounds; the "candle money," which was collected from individuals making votive offerings; and donations to the Society of St. Vincent DePaul, a Catholic charity committed to helping the poor.

Rood was also responsible for making entries in ledgers and tally sheets which were maintained by the parish to keep track of the donations received.
*Reprinted with permission from *Lowellsun.com.*

Commentary: When investigators researched Rood's bank records, they discovered a striking pattern of cash deposits, as much as $1,500 at a time, immediately following Sunday services. The investigation revealed that Rood had no visible source of legitimate cash income. She was paid for her church duties exclusively by check.

The parish priest noticed there was a problem when he personally and privately counted the candle and parish offertory collection and found it totaled $127. When Rood counted the same money the next day, she made a written report stating the total was only $97.

The following week, the parish priest and other parishioners conducted their own private count of the donated funds before Rood submitted her figures. Rood's figures, submitted in written form, reflected substantially lower amounts, and several large bills that had been specifically noted by the priest were missing.

***

Toledo Blade

January 12, 2012
(Originally reported 2010)

Employee Indicted in Theft from Nonprofit*

By Errica Blake

An employee of St. Paul's Community Center, who for five years worked with the organization's clientele to help them stay financially stable, faces charges that she stole thousands of dollars over several years from the group.

Lisa Duda, 39, of Temperance, was indicted by a Lucas County grand jury Friday and charged with aggravated theft.

She is accused of stealing more than $204,000, from October 2005 through September 2009, while employed with the nonprofit organization that offers transitional housing and mental health services for the homeless and indigent.

If convicted, she faces up to five years in prison.

"It was a sucker punch. No one saw it coming," said Anthony Thiros, president of the St. Paul's board of directors.

"But nonetheless, some irregularities came to light in September," Mr. Thiros said.

An employee at a bank with which the organization works noticed $700 checks regularly being written from the account. Mr. Thiros said, "the suspicions were brought to St. Paul's officials, who questioned the staff and contacted authorities.

Ms. Duda is charged with writing checks for money that was in the account as reserves. According to police, she wrote checks for personal use, including for household expenses.

*Reprinted with the permission of the *Toledo Blade*.

Commentary: The stolen money was returned to the clients from other investments held by St. Paul Community Center. St. Paul's has a program in which they assist mentally disabled clients to handle their bills. The money was stolen from reserve funds connected to that program. As a part of her plea bargain, Duda agreed to pay back the money.

CHAPTER SIX
Thievery Currents Strengthen
2011

With USCCB action serving little more than *window dressing,* reports of thievery continued to flourish at all levels making 2011 no different than before, except there was more.

Two smaller cases gained attention on the East Coast. Both were examples of the congregations placing sole financial responsibility in *the priest's* hands without ensuring proper safeguards. In Garnerville, New York, the pastor at Rockland County Roman Catholic Church was charged with one count of third-degree grand larceny for stealing $25,000 from the Church to pay for personal expenses, including online gambling.

In a more substantial case, the pastor of St. Vincent de Paul Parish in Stirling, New Jersey, received a prison sentence for tax evasion. Just three days after becoming pastor of the parish, he opened a personal account at the local bank which became the conduit for him to deposit church monies that were used for personal expenses. He misdirected funds from the parish's cemetery account, its school account, and even donations. He solicited funds for two families he invented as Hurricane Katrina victims and provided updates on the fictitious families' recovery from the disaster.

The FBI finally determined he'd stolen nearly $64,000 which was used to purchase family Christmas and birthday presents among other things and to take trips to Vail, Colorado, Hawaii, and Ireland. In addition to paying back the stolen funds, the priest had to pay back taxes, was assessed a $30,000 fine, and served five months of prison time with two years of supervised home-release, including a period of home confinement.

The totals for notable cases made a significant leap in 2011, increasing more than $600,000 over 2010. The large attention-getting cases were missing, but they were replaced by seven thefts in the range between $300,000 and $650,000.

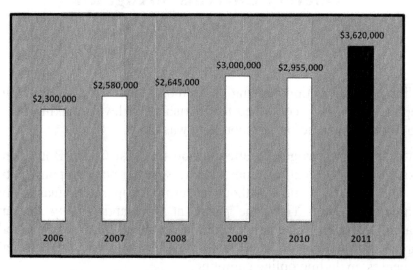

Chart 6 — Thievery Currents Strengthen

Two cases received national media attention in 2011. In Pennsylvania, another flamboyant priest lived the good life, eating at the finest restaurants and traveling around the world. In Nevada, the priest of a 7,000-family congregation was the opposite — low-key and not outgoing. He knowingly submitted fraudulent annual reports to the archdiocese's office in San Francisco, across state lines, for which he would be found guilty of mail fraud.

Former Reading Priest Charged with Embezzling over $400,000*

February 10, 2011

Police in Berks County on Wednesday arrested former pastor, Rev. John Nachjski, for embezzling more than $475,000 from local churches.

YORK, PA — A former priest of St. Joseph and St. Stanislaus Catholic churches was arrested by police in Berks County on Wednesday. The Rev. John Nachjski has been charged with embezzling money from the Reading churches where he was pastor for more than 15 years

The Berks County District Attorney's Office said Nachajski used funds left to the church by two deceased parishioners and wrote checks with church funds payable to himself. In addition, he purchased a timeshare in Mexico.

Nachajski, 64, pastor at St. Anthony of Padua Church in Reading from 1992 to 2009, was arraigned before District Judge Stuart D. Kennedy on the theft charges and released on $25,000 unsecured bail.

He was charged with theft by failure to make required disposition of funds received, theft by deception, theft by unlawful taking or disposition, receiving stolen property, forgery and securing execution of documents by deception.

Officials said the Diocese of Allentown contacted the Berks County District Attorney's Office after an audit completed at the church in November 2009 revealed the missing funds.

Police said the audit review showed Nachajski was involved in suspicious purchases, transactions, and transfers and that funds were unaccounted for. An unknown bank account was also revealed. Nachajski stole the money left to the church by two deceased parishioners by making a series of transfers to accounts only he knew about and had access to.

Matt Kerr, diocese spokesman, said, "The parish intends to file an insurance claim and expects to be reimbursed for much of the alleged misused money."

* Composite article based upon the stories of 2/9/11 issues of the *Daily News* (Parsippany-Troy Hills, NJ) and *The Morning Call* (Allentown, PA), and the 6/10/11 issue of tnonline.com (*Times News*).

Commentary: The checks Nachajski had signed over to himself went for gourmet food and dining in San Francisco, Jamaica, Aruba, and New York; travel to Thailand, Germany, and the British Virgin Islands. Add to that tanning clubs, limos, and women's apparel and jewelry for his female traveling companion.

Investigators also discovered funds from the wills of deceased parishioners who left money to the Church. He transferred it to accounts under his control and used these funds to purchase a home in New York for his traveling companion, who subsequently became his wife. Later, some of the funds were used for travel companions other than his wife.

***

Las Vegas Priest Pleads Guilty to Stealing $650,000 to Feed Gambling Addiction
October 12, 2011

LAS VEGAS — Father Kevin McAuliffe, 58, pleaded guilty today to three counts of mail fraud for stealing $650,000 from a church. He could face up to 20 years in prison and a $250,000 fine on each count.

McAuliffe, a priest and pastor at St. Elizabeth Ann Seton Church, admitted to stealing from the church from 2002 to 2010. The Reverend took the money over a period of eight years from St. Elizabeth Ann Seton Roman Catholic Church. The money was quietly taken from funds for votive candles, missions, and the gift shop.

McAuliffe also submitted false information to the Las Vegas Diocese that under-represented the church's income in financial reports, according to court records.

U.S. Attorney Bogden said while serving as the vicar general of the Las Vegas Diocese, McAuliffe hid his moves by under-reporting the income of the parish. He was privy to the finances of the diocese as he was a signatory to the financial statements of 2008, 2009, and 2010, which were sent to the Catholic Archdiocese in San Francisco.

McAuliffe also used church funds to reimburse personal expenses made on his credit card, much of which was to pay his gambling expenses. When his video poker addiction was revealed, church parishioners were ready to forgive McAuliffe.

"The diocese and parish have been cooperating fully with federal authorities," diocese Bishop Joseph Pepe said in a statement. He said the church administrators were "fully engaged in the handling of this matter internally."

* Composite article based upon the stories of 10/7/11 in the issue of the *Las Vegas Sun,* in the of 10/9/11 issue *Las Vegas Review-Journal,* and the 10/12/11 issue of *The Christian Post.*

Commentary: It's a hard lesson to learn without having proper procedures in place and following them. Thievery can happen anywhere, even in a pious environment. The Diocese now has the proper safeguards in place. The worst aspect of Father McAuliffe's transgressions is he knowingly signed and submitted false financial statements in the annual statements *mailed* to the Archdiocese office in San Francisco, leading to the mail fraud charges.

***

Wisconsin State Journal
February 22, 2011

Former Watertown Priest Sentenced for Stealing Church Funds, Defrauding Parishioners*
By Doug Erickson

JEFFERSON, WI — A former Watertown priest convicted of stealing church funds and defrauding parishioners apologized to his congregation at his sentencing Tuesday, saying he hurt people "terribly, though totally unintentionally."

The Rev. Thomas Marr, 66, who led St. Bernard's Catholic Church in Watertown for 24 years, was spared prison, but sentenced to nine months in a county jail as a condition of a seven-year probationary period.

About two dozen supporters filled the courtroom, including longtime parishioner Mary Wagner, who told Jefferson County Circuit Judge Jacqueline Erwin that Marr is a wonderful priest, but that "finance is not his cup of tea and never has been."

Marr was accused of soliciting money from dozens of parishioners and friends and turning it over — perhaps as much as $613,000 — to a friend, Arthur Eith, who claimed to be awaiting a huge payout on a Nigerian business venture. Eith allegedly promised Marr a $1 million donation to St. Bernard's.

Marr pled guilty in December to two felony counts of theft. Eith remains under investigation by the state Department of Justice and has repeatedly declined comment.

Reprinted with permission from the Wisconsin State Journal.

Commentary: Marr read a brief statement asking forgiveness for those he hurt. "I have no excuses for my bad judgment," he said. A member of the congregation said he was not speaking for the Church, but for himself and those who had left St. Bernard's or have become "disgusted" with the Church over how things were handled.

Judge Erwin said she considered Marr's age, decades of good character, and lack of a prior record. She said she has little concern he will steal again, but that jail time was necessary to deter others. After three months in jail, Marr could apply for an alternative restriction, such as electronic monitoring. He will be required to pay restitution to St. Bernard's and over $134,000 to 17 households. Many other victims did not seek repayment and were not part of the court's order.

***

Bishop Blasts Former Priest Accused of Embezzling*

July 19, 2011

Parishioners of St. Leo's Catholic Church in Bonita Springs, Florida, learn new details of the church's final financial reports.

BONITA SPRINGS, FL — Bishop of the Diocese of Venice says in a letter to the congregation that Father Strycharz was allegedly caught stealing a lot of money, as reported by an independent accounting firm. These allegations are some of many that have placed him on administrative leave.

Strycharz, who led the church for five years through tremendous growth in parishioners and a multimillion-dollar expansion, has remained quiet, his supporters claim, because of a gag ordered placed on him by the Diocese. His supporters banded together to form "Save the Diocese of Southwest Florida" and have been raising money to defend him.

The released audit of church finances, conducted over most of a year by the accounting firm of Larson Allen, LLP., shows $1 million is unaccounted for, including $665,000 used to pay Father Strycharz's personal credit cards and over $170,000 used to pay educational expenses for the children of a former business manager.

The letter goes on to allege nepotism, saying the father of the former business manager received $45,000 as an advisor. And the parish also paid almost $150,000 to a painting service which was owned by Father Strycharz's brother.

*Composite article based upon the stories on 6/17/11 on NBC 2 First, and stories in the 6/17/11 issue of the *Naples Daily News,* and he 6/19/11 issue of *The News-Press* (Fort Myers).

Commentary: Legal charges were not filed, and the matter was handled by the bishop. The spokesperson for the Diocese of Venice indicated Father Strycharz refused to cooperate and offered no explanation for the expenses. He was placed on leave by the Church and later defrocked.

***

Courier-Post

August 4, 2011

Priest Charged with Stealing $305K*

Bank tipped police on suspicious activity.

WILMINGTON, DE — For the second time in six months, the *Courier-Post* reports a Roman Catholic priest is facing felony theft charges in New Castle County Superior Court.

According to the *Courier-Post,* a New Castle County Grand Jury this week indicted the Rev. Michael Angeloni on charges that he stole $305,000 from an elderly female parishioner.

The Delaware Attorney General's office said Wednesday that an arrest warrant has been issued for 62-year-old Angeloni, who is not yet in custody, on one count of theft of more than $100,000.

Prosecutors said the indictment comes after a five-month investigation by the Delaware Attorney General's Senior Protection Initiative.

The *Courier-Post* indicated Angeloni is accused of soliciting money on multiple occasions from a woman — a parishioner at Church of the Holy Child (Brandywood) on Naamaus Road — where Angeloni had served as an associate pastor.

Prosecutors said Angeloni told the victim he needed the money for certain, specific personal expenses, "when in fact, the money was used for other purposes."

Prosecutors did not explain what those "other purposes" were — or the personal expenses — but said they were tipped off to the problem by Wilmington Trust, which reported suspicious financial activity on the victim's account. Court papers indicate the thefts of the funds occurred between August of 2008 and February 2011 and that the victim was over the age of 62.

*Reprinted in accordance with "fair use" guidelines.

Commentary: Angeloni had a sense of humor and plenty of jokes for the congregation. He was so well liked; the bishop sent a letter to the membership encouraging them to attend his last Mass so they could wish him well. But beneath this persona, was a conniving man who took advantage of his personality to scam others.

A woman's trust in him led to a series of withdrawals from her bank account. Fortunately for her, a close friend at the bank noticed what she knew to be unusual withdrawals and tipped off the police.

***

Leesville Daily Leader
November 25, 2011

Natchitoches Parish Priest Arrested for Theft*

A priest from Natchitoches Parish was arrested Tuesday by Louisiana State Police for theft exceeding $250,000.

A priest from Natchitoches Parish was arrested Tuesday by Louisiana State Police for theft exceeding $250,000, according to the *Leesville Daily Leader*.

James A. Foster, 66, was arrested and charged with one count of theft exceeding $250,000 as a result of a state police investigation, the *Daily Leader* reported.

According to the state police, Foster, who was the pastor at the Basilica of the Immaculate Conception Catholic Church in Natchitoches, served as the pastor of the parish and used parish funds to issue checks to himself and deprive the parish and diocese of funds. Between January 2008 and when he was arrested, police say he obtained over $250,000 from parish funds.

State police initiated an investigation after a request was received from the Catholic Diocese of Alexandria. The record shows, after his arrest, Foster was booked into the Natchitoches Parish Detention Center.
*Reprinted in accordance with "fair use" guidelines.

Commentary: The priest had issued checks to himself and used the Church's corporate credit card to purchase personal items. The diocese was open and transparent in the legal proceedings, but once again, had failed to ensure that funds at the parish were *handled in a proper manner.*

***

Three cases were identified — in Wisconsin, Illinois, and California — where staff members were not properly supervised, and one individual had sole access to church funds. In each of these cases, the persons involved were long-term, well-respected individuals. Finally, close follow-up by a second party uncovered the schemes that had been employed.

***

Journal Sentinel
December 27, 2011

Church Secretary Charged with Embezzling from Oak Creek Parish*

The *Journal Sentinel* reported a church secretary was charged Tuesday with embezzling more than $200,000 from her Oak Creek congregation.

The Milwaukee County district attorney's office accused Darlene Vodvarka, 57, of stealing $217,483 over seven years from St. Matthew Catholic Church.

Vodvarka, who worked for the church for about 14 years, is charged with two counts of felony theft of more than $10,000. If convicted of both counts, she could be sentenced to up to 20 years in prison and fined up to $50,000, according to the *Journal Sentinel.*

A church official had confirmed in September that a theft investigation was underway and that a staff member had been placed on administrative leave. The church's finance committee had contacted police after uncovering accounting

irregularities over the summer, church treasurer Mike Kuick said.

According to the criminal complaint, the scheme involved payments for "scrip," gift cards that merchants had donated to St. Matthew to sell to raise money for its school.
*Reprinted in accordance with "fair use" guidelines.

Commentary: In charge of collecting money from parishioners and students for scrip, Vodvarka was responsible for depositing that money in the Church's account.

Vodvarka bought large quantities of the fundraising gift cards for herself that totaled over $225,000. She gave those checks to the volunteer, who recorded the amounts and gave the checks back to her to deposit. But most of Vodvarka's checks never made it to the bank; slightly more than $8,000 of the checks were deposited, allowing her to pocket the difference.

Vodvarka covered up the fraud by falsifying the Church's books. For example, tuition payments were recorded correctly in the Church's accounts for each family. That turned out to be the key to uncovering the embezzlement scheme.

***

Daily Herald
February 7, 2011

West Chicago Deacon Gets Six Years for Embezzlement*
By Josh Stockinger

The former deacon and business manager at a Roman Catholic parish in West Chicago was sentenced Monday to six years in prison for embezzling more than $317,000 from the church.

George Valdez, 58, admitted in a plea agreement to writing unauthorized checks to himself and transferring money from the St. Mary's Parish bank account into his own. He also used

a parish credit card for personal expenses and failed to pay for a family insurance policy.

Assistant State's Attorney Helen Kapas-Erdman said Valdez used the ill-gotten funds to pay for White Sox and Bears tickets, expensive dinners, hotel stays, and his daughter's wedding. The thefts from 2006 to 2009 were uncovered during a financial audit.

"For more than three years, Mr. Valdez stole from those who had placed their trust and confidence in him," DuPage County State's Attorney Robert Berlin said. "He betrayed that trust by lining his own pockets with funds donated to the parish."

*Reprinted with permission from the *Daily Herald.*

Commentary: Within three months of being hired, Valdez turned to stealing. At a court hearing attended by several members of his family, he fought back tears as he apologized to God, his family, and his church.

"He's a good man who did something wrong," defense attorney Nicholas Kirkeles said. "He wanted to provide things for his family and just wasn't able to do it. He made a mistake and it started compounding."

The Diocese of Joliet, which is self-insured, reimbursed St. Mary's Parish for its losses, and immediately added two auditors to the central office staff.

***

Danville Patch
May 2, 2011

Three Charged with Embezzling from St. Isidore Church; $580,000 Missing*

A nine-month police investigation led to the arrest of two of the Danville parish's employees and one parish volunteer, the Danville Patch reported.

After a nine-month police investigation, the Contra Costa County (CA) District Attorney's Office filed charges Monday against three people it says embezzled a total of $580,000 from the church in Danville, according to the *Danville Patch*.

Danville Police Chief Steve Simpkins said the investigation found that former St. Isidore employees Kathleen Dake and Virgilio Lukban and volunteer Evelyn Peinado stole about $360,000 from the church through fraudulent use of credit cards.

Dake also is charged in connection with stealing about $220,000 more, using checks from St. Isidore for personal expenses.
*Reprinted in accordance with "fair use" guidelines.

Commentary: Dake was an office manager who began working at the Church in 2002, and Lukban was a facilities manager hired in 2003.

The diocese admitted the parish did not have proper internal controls in place to detect and prevent such a high-level, sophisticated crime. In the aftermath, the parish did what it should have done in the first place; segregating the financial duties by hiring a bookkeeper and a separate accounting manager to handle cash receipts, disbursements, payroll, and financial statement preparation.

CHAPTER SEVEN
Tributaries Grow and Millions Flow
2012

With concern growing over the number of Catholics no longer engaged, the Church came front and center. In his Ash Wednesday homily, Pope Francis said, "Lent is the perfect time to let go of selfish and indifferent attitudes... returning to God with one's entire heart is not something external, but instead comes from the depth of ourselves."

Empty Pews Study

In March, a major conference focused on issues confronting the Catholic membership. At the "Lapsed Catholic" Conference, Charles Zech presented findings from a survey he'd co-authored, "Empty Pews." Trying to understand why so many Catholics had stopped attending Mass, Zech reported his findings from a 16-question survey of nearly 300 parishioners in the Diocese of Trenton.

While the study was limited to one diocese, it likely could have come from anywhere in the country. Its findings paralleled a 2007 Pew Foundation report, which noted one-third of Americans were raised Catholic and one-third of those had left the Church. Responses from the participants ranged far and wide — from the "priest who crowned himself king and looks down on all" to the Church's stance on homosexuality, birth control, women priests, and how the Church handled the sex abuse scandal and accountability of church leaders.

Zech pointed out the recent results could be divided into two categories: "Things that can't change, but that we can do a better job of explaining." and "Things that aren't difficult to fix." He pointed out the Church isn't likely to change its stance on such issues as birth control or celibacy any time soon, but dioceses could change the way they explain certain doctrines and train pastors.

Criticism of the sex abuse scandal was predictable. Zech pointed out, "That doesn't surprise anybody. They did not manage that well, and they are still not managing it well… it hasn't gone away."

Vatican Synod — Lapsed Catholics

In October, a select group of 250 bishops and other high-ranking prelates met for three weeks in Rome to address the lapsed Catholic issue. The synod was seen as an entity that would not develop any broad-based top-down strategies, but outcomes were not to be taken lightly. The magnitude of the issue was pointed out in an interview by Louisville Archbishop Joseph E. Kurtz, "We're having the meeting 'not because it's a new gospel — it's the same gospel of Jesus Christ…' what is new is the 'focus on those 1/8 whose faith has grown tepid.'"

The official working document for the synod suggested focusing mainly on re-evangelizing Catholics who have lost faith, rather than on those who had exited to other Christian denominations. But Reverend Thomas Reese, a senior fellow at Georgetown University's Woodstock Theological Center, said the synod is handicapped by a growing divide between Catholic theologians and bishops over where to draw the line between what a Catholic must believe and legitimate areas where people can question and dissent.

When it recognized the scope of the growing problem, the synod made an important contribution for the future — *recognition of a problem* is the first step in solving an issue!

***

The dollar impact of notable cases increased $175,000 more than in 2011, but the profile of cases in 2012 was much different. In 2011, the preponderance of cases centered in the mid-range — $250,000 to $650,000. Interestingly, the cases in 2012 either hovered around a million dollars or were closer to a hundred thousand dollars.

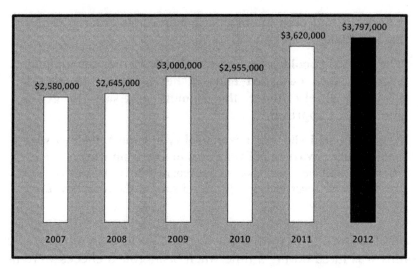

Chart 7 — Tributaries Grow and Millions Slow

***

Judge Slams Woman for 'Outrageous' $1M Theft from Archdiocese∗
October 11, 2012

An angry judge sentenced an elderly, Madam-Alexander-doll-obsessed embezzler to at least four and half years for stealing $1 million from the Archdiocese of New York.

He called her action, "outrageous!"

Anita Colling, 69, of Schulyerville in The Bronx, purchased pricey Madam Alexanders dolls, Belleek China, furniture from Bloomingdales, and clothes from Brook Brothers with the money.

Described as a devout churchgoer, the white-haired matronly-dressed woman said, "No," and shook her head when asked if she could explain why she had looted the church.

"You were put in a position of trust," said Manhattan Supreme Court Justice Lewis Bart Stone. "You stole $1 million. That is an outrageous amount."

He reminded her that this was not the first time she'd been caught. In 1999, she ripped off $46,000 from a temp agency

where she had been the bookkeeper and was ordered to pay back $10,000.

The geriatric bookkeeper cut 458 checks for her son's phony expenses, then deposited them in her account. She always kept the checks under the amount necessary to get a supervisor's approval.

Neighbors said she was never flashy, but the $50,000-a-year bookkeeper always took livery cars to and from work.

*Composite article based upon stories reported in the 1/30/12 issue of the *New York Times* and the 10/11/12 issues of the *New York Daily News* and *New York Post.*

Commentary: Trust, trust, trust… runs throughout this case. Ms. Collins was hired during a time when background checks were not required, so church officials were not aware she'd been convicted of grand larceny for another job and had pleaded guilty to a misdemeanor in another case. She held herself out to be a religious woman, going to church every day; all the time, she was lying and stealing. She issued four hundred and sixty-eight checks from the archdiocese to "KB Collins," the initials of one of her sons. After each check was printed, she would change internal records to show that the check had been issued to a legitimate vendor.

In addition to the expensive dolls, Collins also purchased $18,000 in furniture from Bloomingdale's, $37,000 in clothes from Barneys and Brooks Brothers, and $19,000 in goods from an Irish gift shop.

***

National Catholic Reporter
August 27, 2012

Ex-CFO in Philadelphia Archdiocese Gets Two to Seven Years for Stealing $900,000*
By Matthew Gambino

PHILADELPHIA -- The former chief financial officer of the Archdiocese of Philadelphia will spend the next two to seven years in state prison for embezzling more than $900,000 from the church over seven years.

Common Pleas Court Judge Ellen Ceisler sentenced Anita Guzzardi, 44, to prison at a hearing Aug. 24 in Philadelphia on her third-degree felony conviction of theft by deception. Guzzardi will also serve seven years of probation on two other convictions, forgery and unlawful use of a computer. She had pleaded guilty to the three charges July 29.

Guzzardi sat downcast in a black business suit as Assistant District Attorney Lisa Caulfield described what she called the "lavish lifestyle" Guzzardi lived fueled by funds she embezzled from her work as a trusted senior financial officer of the archdiocese.

Beginning in late 2004, Caulfield said, Guzzardi began to write archdiocesan checks to cover her expenses on her American Express credit card. The deception grew to a second Amex card and a Chase card, expenses she covered by cutting more than 300 checks over time, totaling $906,000.

Those expenses included frequent business trips in which she included family and friends, plus vacations to Hawaii, Las Vegas, the Bahamas, and other locales, and shopping sprees for clothes, gifts, and flowers for herself, family, and friends.

*Reprinted with permission of National Catholic Reporter Publishing Company, Kansas, City, MO. NCRonline.org.

Commentary: No one knew Ms. Guzzardi spent her free time playing the slots at the Borgata Hotel Casino & Spa in Atlantic City and enjoying vacations at expensive getaways using her American Express card. Her scam unraveled when a fraud investigator with American Express wondered why the archdiocese was ringing up charges at a casino. Ms. Guzzardi had check-signing authority and sent the checks to American Express.

Individuals in the archdiocese expressed shock and dismay — "she knew her stuff, knew what she was talking about" — came from all of those interviewed. Clearly, her competency overwhelmed those responsible for the checks and balances, which were not put into use.

In fact, as it turned out, it was found that "the archdiocese for years held its finances in strict secrecy… the Archdiocese of Philadelphia was abysmal in terms of financial transparency and accountability."

***

National Catholic Reporter
November 2012

Embezzlement, a Suicide, and St. John's University*
By Tom Gallagher

The most sordid case of embezzlement is without question the case of Cecilia Chang, a 30-year employee and dean at the Vincentian-run St. John's University in Queens, New York.

Chang, 59, was facing two 205-count indictments and was in the middle of one trial in Brooklyn federal court for accusations of stealing more than $1 million from the university.

One report noted "there was virtually no oversight of her activities by the former school President, the Rev. Joseph Cahill, who is dead, or the current President Donald Harrington."

A Vincentian priest, Harrington regularly accepted luxurious travel arrangements made by Chang and lavish personal gifts from her.

The *New York Post* had this to say about the extraordinary gift-giving by Chang: "Chang had lavished gifts on many officials, later submitting phony invoices for reimbursement, according to testimony. The biggest beneficiary was the university's president, the Rev. Donald Harrington, who later testified against her. She provided him with more than forty custom-made suits from Hong Kong, along with pricey Patek Philippe watches and lavish stays at The Four Seasons hotel in Hawaii, according to testimony."

On the witness stand, however, Harrington amazingly remembered things differently: He was "uncomfortable" and didn't remember important facts from days gone by. Funny how that works — and convenient, too.

Incredibly, and against her lawyer's counsel, Chang took the witness stand in her own defense.

"Chang essentially conceded to jurors that she'd lied on tax returns and to the FBI about some $1 million she was accused of embezzling from the Queens Catholic University — and the sometimes loud defensive testimony was repeatedly interrupted by the judge's admonitions and courtroom laughter, and her contentious shouts of 'No!'" reported *The New Post.*

*Reprinted with permission of the National Catholic Reporter Publishing Company, Kansas, City, MO. NCRonline.org.

Commentary: A day after her testimony, the trial ended abruptly — Chang committed suicide. The judge characterized the trial like "a Shakespearean tragedy." She may have been the greatest con artist in Catholic history.

***

The following cases illustrate again, and again, the importance of having appropriate controls and procedures in place. That way the bully won't prevail, the "seemingly" nice person with a pleasant personality and a smile won't win out, and the person who outright lies won't get away with the cash.

Checks and balances must win out over "trust."

MLive.com
Michigan News
March 10, 2012

Former Northern Michigan Catholic School Principal Accused of Embezzling $100,000 Pleads Guilty to a Lesser Charge*
By Heidi Fenton

CHARLEVOIX, MI— A former elementary school principal pleaded guilty Friday to two counts of embezzlement stemming from allegations she took about $100,000 from a Catholic school.

Keisha Veryser, 36, of Hayes Township, was ordered to pay $75,000 in restitution — $37,500 at the time of her sentencing — under terms of a plea agreement.

Veryser originally was charged with a seven-count felony warrant that included two counts of perjury for allegedly making incorrect statements under oath during civil proceedings.

Authorities said Veryser, a principal at St. Mary Elementary School, started embezzling $100,000 about one month after she assumed the position. Veryser resigned in March 2010 and was arrested on Nov. 1, 2011.

*Reprinted with permission of MLive.com and Barcroft Studios.

Commentary: Veryser was sentenced on two counts of embezzlement, each a 5-year sentence for taking $1,000 to $20,000 from a non-profit organization. The first half of her restitution will be given to the Catholic Diocese and the remaining may be at the discretion of the organization.

***

WTAE
Pittsburgh Action 4 News
April 18, 2012

Priest Accused of Stealing $140,000 Pleads Guilty*

SWISSVALE, PA — The Allegheny County district attorney says a priest charged with stealing over $140,000 from his parish between 1999 and 2009 has pleaded guilty to theft.

WTAE Action News reports, in exchange for his plea on Wednesday, the Rev. Francis Drabiska was sentenced to seven years of probation and ordered to pay restitution of more than $140,000.

According to WTAE Action News, Drabiska, 61, resigned from Word of God Parish in 2010, and *allegedly admitted the theft* to church authorities, but the amount wasn't mentioned at that time.

Auditors for the Catholic Diocese of Pittsburgh were suspicious of missing collection money in 2005 because the count of loose cash was low, according to a criminal complaint filed by the district attorney's office.

"That parish was not using tamper-proof bags, which every parish is supposed to use," the Rev. Ron Lengwin, a diocesan spokesman, told Channel 4 Action News in September 2011.

According to the complaint, auditors did a "cash drop audit test" using six $10 bills at different Masses and recorded the serial numbers of each bill. When the collection money was counted, three of the six bills were missing.

The complaint alleged that Drabiska had been warned of his extravagant spending by church officials and that he admitted the money was used for a lifestyle beyond his means.
*Reprinted in accordance with "fair use" guidelines.

Commentary: Father Drabiska had several high-balance credit cards and used money taken from the parish collections to pay toward those. A Macy's credit card, which he used to buy designer sportswear, sheets, dinnerware, and cosmetics, had a balance of more than $5,000.

***

MLive.com
Grand Rapids News
October 1, 2012

Wyoming Church Embezzler Spent Stolen Money at Strip Clubs, Gambling∗
By Heidi Fenton

KENT COUNTY, MI — Speaking about countless people in Kent County and beyond who have gone without charity assistance from a financially-burdened Wyoming parish, a judge exceeded state guidelines when sentencing a man accused of embezzling thousands to spend on gambling and strip clubs.

James Kulfan, 55, will spend eight to 20 years in prison for taking at least $135,000 from St. John Vianney Catholic Church from late 2009 through late 2011. He will serve another five to 10-year prison term at the same time for taking nearly $20,000 from Grandville-based Dymo Ministries.

Kulfan's attorney, Frank Stanley, spoke of his client's remorse and decision to plead guilty to both charges of embezzlement, taking full responsibility for his actions. Kulfan, he said, had prayed about his situation, was a "new man," and had "turned his life around." The statements were met with a chorus of hushed questions from those present in the gallery.

The Rev. Michael Alber told the court what his parish had endured through its financial troubles. Staff members were eliminated due to lack of funding. Giving to international charities all but ceased, he said. Thousands of dollars in spending cuts were made, but the money kept coming up short. "Jim always had answers for us, but his answers never seemed to materialize," Alber said.

"Kulfan controlled and bullied staff so they wouldn't question," Alber told the judge. "Jim made it very clear he was in control."

*Reprinted with permission of MLive.com and Barcroft Studios.

Commentary: At the trial, Rev. Michael told the court he could "understand and sympathize" with a person if the goal was to put food on the table and a roof over his head. But, he said, Jim Kulfan used the money to "live a sordid life in strip clubs." The judge called Kulfan's behavior "outrageous."

CHAPTER EIGHT
Turbulent Waters Slow
2013

Much has been written about how to prevent stealing from the weekly collection plate and church fraud. Michael W. Ryan has repeatedly made the point — by providing examples of how to achieve a secure collection-to-bank process, by sending letters to individual bishops appealing to them to enforce Canon Law, and by publishing a book, *"NONFEASANCE,"* on the failures of the Church to protect its primary source of income.

Yet, it continues to happen and most of the time it doesn't get reported. Two articles published in 2013 provide further insights into the magnitude of the problem.

Referring to *The Washington Post* investigation of fraud in nonprofit organizations, Walter Pavlo (32) reemphasized that "incidents are either not reported at all, or reported, but not directly to authorities... bad news, like 'theft,' does not sit well with contributors... as much as 95 percent of fraud within churches goes undetected or unreported." Further, he pointed out that unlike other organizations, "churches are not required to do an annual report" — they are excluded from all IRS requirements.

Barry Bowen (2) put church thievery into context:

One of the dirty secrets of Christianity is that there are numerous crooked pastors, priests and church financial secretaries embezzling funds. The International Bulletin of Missionary Research projected that $37 billion would be stolen by Christian religious leaders in 2013 and this fraud will reach $60 billion annually by 2025.

Based on these projections, the amount stolen each year by Christian leaders increases *annually* at a rate of $2B per year.

***

The total dollar amount recorded for the notable cases in 2013 dropped significantly below the amount recorded in 2012, declining by almost $800,000. The total for 2013 was $3,005,000 — still a sizable amount.

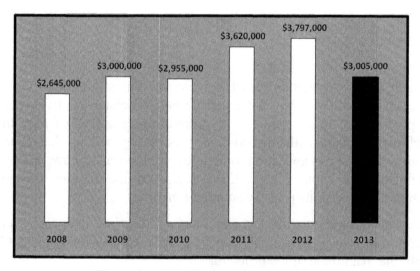

Chart 8 — Turbulent Waters Slow

***

20 Years Possible for Catholic Credit Union Manager for Embezzling $2.1M*
January 21, 2013

MONROE, MI — Sharon Broadway stole $2.1 million from the United Catholic Credit Union over a long time, and she'll spend a long time in prison. The 62-year-old Toledo, Ohio woman was sentenced January 17, to 10 to 240 months for embezzling $2.1 million since 1958 from the credit union in Temperance, Michigan.

Monroe County Circuit Judge Michael A. Weiport, sentenced Broadway to concurrently serve 45 months to 240 months for racketeering, ordered her to pay $2.5 million in restitution to

NCUA, and barred her from working in the financial industry.

The credit union was closed in August when problems were detected. Because of insurance, no depositor lost money.

As manager, secretary, board member, and sole employee of the credit union, Broadway was able to conceal her crimes for years using a complex money laundering scheme involving forged checks and multiple aliases, according to Michigan Attorney General Bill Schuette.

Broadway used the embezzled funds for her personal use, authorities said. She spent some of the money on others. "There really is nothing to show for it. She didn't live an extravagant life," her lawyer said.

Investigators say Broadway hid her scheme by not recording certificates of deposit on credit union books. Prosecutors say the embezzlement was discovered during a routine examination by regulators.

*Composite article based upon stories reported in the 1/18/03 issue of *Crain's Detroit Business* and on CBS News Detroit, and in the 1/21/03 issue of the *Credit Union Times*.

Commentary: Broadway was a one-person operation — there were no controls or checks and balances — as a result, she was able to conceal her crimes for years using a complex money laundering scheme involving forged checks and multiple aliases. Her fraud was uncovered after a routine examination by the Michigan Office of Financial and Insurance Regulation revealed that a substantial number of certificates of deposit went unrecorded.

Defense lawyer Lorin Zaner told *The Blade* of Toledo that Broadway is "very apologetic for what happened and how she's let so many people down." While that is a matter of public record, it seems hard to believe — scheming for 20 years sounds more like she meant 'if they wouldn't have caught me, I wouldn't have let you down.'

Depositors at the credit union were a product of trickle-down faith-management — meaning they transported their values and trust learned in the Church to other church-related entities.

The Mercury
April 19, 2013

PA Priest Sentenced for Taking $380K from Parish*

GETTYSBURG, PA – According to *The Mercury*, Adams County Judge Michael George sentenced a Catholic priest in central Pennsylvania to 11½ to 23 months behind bars for stealing more than $380,000 from his parish.

Judge George indicated that 52-year-old former pastor Caesar Belchez transferred more than $190,000 from various accounts at St. Joseph the Worker Parish in Bonneauville to an online stock account, and more than $120,000 to a personal account.

Judge George ordered Belchez at Thursday's hearing to also make full restitution and serve 12 years of probation. Court records indicate he is eligible for work release while serving his sentence.

*Reprinted in accordance with "fair use" guidelines.

Commentary: All parishes and schools in the Diocese of Harrisburg are required to have insurance, so the impact of the theft on parish services was limited. While the parish had proper controls in place, the irregularities were found by a new priest. It's a good reminder, even with the best procedures, "each" individual with oversight must pay careful attention to the details.

The diocese maintains a zero-tolerance policy toward all financial malpractice, and after validation, matters are automatically turned over to civil authorities.

***

MLive.com
Muskegon News
April 29, 2013

Grand Haven Catholic Deacon Sentenced to Jail for Stealing $120,000 from St. Patrick's Collection Plates*

By John S. Hausman

GRAND HAVEN, MI — Joseph Thomas Finnigan, the 73-year-old Catholic deacon who admitted stealing $120,000 from Grand Haven collection plates over some five years, will spend the next year of his life in jail and the rest of his life trying to pay back the money.

Ottawa County Circuit Judge Jon Hulsing's words and sentence Monday, April 29, were stern. The jail term — one year with no work release — exceeded the request of the Ottawa County Prosecutor's Office for 10 months of jail and no work release for the first six months. It was more than six times the 60-day jail sentence recommended by the pre-sentence investigator.

Hulsing also placed Finnigan on probation for four years, ordered him to serve 250 hours of community service, and pay restitution of $120,000, minus $2,500 Finnigan has already paid. He also must pay fees and costs.

Finnigan told the judge he had expected a brother-in-law to pay the $120,000 by sentencing date, but that relative decided not to do so. In answer to the judge's question, Finnigan acknowledged that the $2,500 already paid also was not his own money, and that he had not yet divested assets to begin making restitution, although, he said, that is "pending."

Finnigan pleaded guilty March 1 to two counts of larceny of more than $20,000. At that time the prosecutor's office dropped a count of embezzlement of more than $20,000. Originally that was on the condition that Finnigan repay the full amount by the time of sentencing, but the prosecutor opted to stick with the plea agreement because the facts of the case fit the larceny charge better than the embezzlement

charge, according to Senior Attorney Karen Miedema of the prosecutor's office.

*Reprinted with permission of MLive.com and Barcroft Studios.

Commentary: Noting that Finnigan, in a letter to the court, had called his crimes "an irrational act," the judge said to him in court, "This was not an irrational act. This was a series of acts you made over a series of years… for financial gain. It's not as if you had a bad day."

An accountant hired by the Church after the thefts came to light concluded that Finnigan "deliberately and painstakingly (evaded) internal controls," taking a great deal of effort to conceal his larceny.

Acknowledging that he had received numerous letters supporting Finnigan by pointing out his good works and his worth as a husband, the judge said: "It has also been said that an individual's true character is revealed in what they do when they think no one is watching."

"I am struggling to understand his behavior," the parish priest said. "From my perspective, he seems to have been manipulative and calculating… in a position of extreme trust… While I forgive him, I cannot condone what he has done to me, his church, fellow parishioners, his family, and his God," the priest told the judge.

***

Cleveland.com
June 24, 2013

Former Romanian Catholic Priest Pleads Guilty to Theft from Church*

CLEVELAND, OH — *Cleveland.com* reported a longtime priest at St. Helena Church on Cleveland's West Side has pleaded guilty to stealing $176,000 from the Romanian Catholic institution, according to a prosecutor.

The Rev. Andre Matthews, 54, used some of the money to pay credit card bills, buy cars, and pay tuition for a family member to attend Cleveland State University, according to Assistant County Prosecutor James Gutierrez.

Gutierrez said some of the money Matthews stole was raised through church-sponsored bingo.

According to *Cleveland.com*, the West 65th Street church is one of several Romanian Catholic churches in Northeast Ohio and has 80 to 100 families as members. It noted that the Rev. Ovidiu Marginean, chancellor at the Romanian Catholic Diocese of Canton, said the services are primarily conducted in Romanian.

Cleveland.com indicated the Romanian Catholic Church recognizes the pope as its leader, but follows different traditions than the Roman Catholic Church, according to the Rev. Cristian Terhes, communications director for the Romanian Catholic Diocese of Canton.

Marginean said Matthews had been pastor at St. Helena for at least 10 years. He left in September 2011.

Matthews' thievery was discovered in 2011, when church leaders noticed some bills were not being paid, Gutierrez said.

The leaders took their concerns to the Prosecutor's Office, Gutierrez said, and the Sheriff's Department investigated.
*Reprinted in accordance with "fair use" guidelines.

Commentary: Investigators plowed through thousands of pages of financial documents and found hundreds of withdrawals by Matthews from the Church's bank account dating back to 2005.

"Matthews was able to deceive his congregation for so long because of his position of trust," the assistant prosecutor said. "People weren't really watching what was going on." The parishioners felt even more betrayed when they learned that Matthews had been secretly married and had two children. A family he supported with their generous donations meant for the betterment of the Church.

Greater distress was added when the parishioners learned that he had been introducing his wife as his cousin, a poor single mother with two children, who eventually became the treasurer for the Church.

***

St. Bernadette Priest Accused of Stealing $230,000 to Feed Gambling Addiction*
October 20, 2013

NORTHBORO, MA — The Pastor of Saint Bernadette Parish has resigned after allegations surfaced that he'd stole more than $200,000 to fuel his gambling addiction.

"It appears that during the last four years, more than $110,000 of school funds and more than $120,000 of parish funds were used by Fr. Gemme for personal expenditures unrelated to the parish or school. As a result of the magnitude of the misuse of funds, the matter has been referred to the District Attorney's Office," McManus wrote to parishioners.

The Rev. Stephen M. Gemme argued for forgiveness. "Human beings are fragile. They fall into sin, they get scared and make choices that are not always good," the 43-year-old priest wrote in a July 28 note in the online newsletter of St. Bernadette Parish. "If there is a person that you need to forgive and you find it hard, please pray for them."

The Rev. Gemme blames the thefts on a gambling addiction, according to Bishop McManus's letter to the diocese, and he is receiving "residential treatment" for it. "If Rev. Gemme truly is suffering from an addiction, then we can all hope that treatment will help him overcome it.

However, an addiction doesn't pardon illegal activity, and Bishop McManus has correctly forwarded the case to the District Attorney.

Legalities aside, an addiction also does not pardon hypocrisy. In the words attributed to Jesus, "Why do you look at the speck of sawdust in your brother's eye and pay no attention to the plank in your own eye? How can you say to your brother, 'Let me take the speck out of your eye,' when all the time there is a plank in your own eye? You hypocrite, first

84

**take the plank out of your own eye, and then you will see
clearly to remove the speck from your brother's eye."**
*Composite article based upon stories reported on 10/12/2013 in the
issue of *Shadow Proof,* on 10/20/2013 in the issue of *The Telegraph &
Gazette Staff,* and on 10/13/2013 on CBS Boston.

Commentary: The thefts went undetected until a member of the
school's advisory board flagged a financial irregularity in a school
account and informed Bishop McManus.

Gemme acknowledged a gambling problem and offered his
resignation, which was accepted. He was also granted a medical
leave of absence and entered residential treatment.

CHAPTER NINE
Thievery Scandal Goes Mainstream
2014

The USCCB remained inactive in terms of gaining control over the thievery problem. It seemed there was a disconnect between the bishops and a growing number of thefts and the escalating amount of dollars being stolen from parishes.

The Pope's leadership and international issues received considerable attention in the media. His tone was coherent and clear. Trying to institute change was not easy. Newspaper headlines seemed more like watching a tennis match between Pope Francis and the Church's nemesis, with the growing number of sex abuse cases being reported, worldwide, compounding the problem.

January 24, 2014

A History of Sexual Abuse by Priests in Chicago Archdiocese

April 11, 2014

Pope Francis Pleas Forgiveness for "Evil" Priests Who Sexually Abused Children

May 7, 2014

Vatican Reveals How Many Priests Defrocked for Sex Abuse Since 2000

May 24, 2014

Pope Francis: Revitalizing the Catholic Church

Throughout the year, Pope Francis' message focused on those who had been chased away from the Catholic Church, especially the young. Following his famous remark, "Who am I to judge?", he called for the church to assist families in better accept their gay and lesbian children. Instead of fighting gay marriage and abortion, he emphasized inequality which he called, "the root of social evil." He revoked the carte blanche authority of bishops to abuse their power and set in motion steps to create greater transparency in the Vatican.

While the Pope was doing a balancing act with worldwide issues, thievery in the US continued to grow. Notable cases rebounded by $300,000 over the 2013 year, suggesting the possibility of a new upward trend. Four cases (each over $425,000) appeared nationwide, in California, Michigan, and Minnesota. Because of the location of these cases, news about them found their way into an increasing number of newspapers.

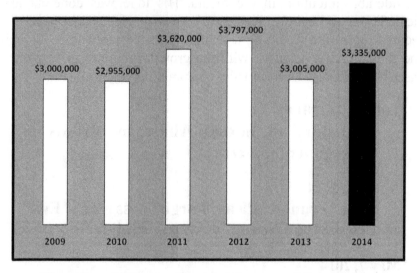

Chart 9 — Thievery Scandal Becomes Mainstream

The first case, covered in detail by Minnesota Public Radio News, provided specific information about the Bishop's cover-up of priests who had one shortcoming or another, including secret accounts used by officials in the Church to cover the costs of misconduct.

On January 23, 2014, *MPR News* published an article entitled "Secret accounts paid for clergy misconduct but left the church open to financial abuse," by Tom Scheck detailing the internal operation of the Archdiocese of St. Paul and Minneapolis. Following a review of thousands of pages of private, internal archdiocese documents, and testimony of an inside informant, the author revealed some of the "common practices" in the Archdiocese of St. Paul and Minneapolis, and in fact, many dioceses across the country.

Scott Domeier, a former top archdiocese accountant, who exploited the secrecy to steal more than $650,000, said, "The clergy misconduct budget was so well concealed that a trained eye wouldn't notice the spending."

Domeier pointed out, Archdiocese leaders made payment decisions with little consideration of how they might hurt the church's budget. Internal financial reports indicated that for years the Archdiocese had diverted millions of dollars away from the main purposes of the Church to deal with clergy misconduct.

Payments associated with clergy misconduct came from separate accounts, depending upon the type of criminal behavior involved. One account paid the costs associated with priests accused of sexually abusing children, while the other was related to the abuse of adults or financial misconduct — each had their own line-item code.

The internal financial reports, from 2002 to 2011, show the Archdiocese used the stealth accounts repeatedly, paying nearly $11 million, about 3 percent of the overall Archdiocese revenues in those years. Essentially, the Archbishop *spent millions of dollars to make the problem go away.*

These funds were used to pay legal fees for the priests, settlements for their victims, the costs of private investigators, and payoffs to priests. On the books, improper behavior was called "Disability" pay; a *"don't ask" culture* kept Archdiocese employees from probing deeper. "Everybody knew not to ask questions," Domeier said.

Domeier indicated the secrecy surrounding church accounts made stealing from them easier. In some cases, he pointed out, "priest support" helped to explain the removal of funds. Domeier pleaded guilty to taking more than $650,000 and was sentenced to a three-year prison term.

***

Catholic News Reporter
May 1, 2014

Suburban Detroit Pastor, Lay Manager Indicted on Federal Fraud Charges*

DETROIT — According to the *Catholic News Reporter,* the suspended pastor of a parish in the Detroit suburbs was indicted April 23 on federal fraud charges, as was the former parish manager of St. Thomas More Parish in Troy.

Father Edward Belczak, 69, who was suspended by the Archdiocese of Detroit in January 2013, was indicted on mail fraud, wire fraud and conspiracy charges in U.S. District Court in Detroit. Janice Verschuren, 67, who left the parish at the time of Father Belczak's suspension, also was named in the 16-page indictment, according to court records.

At issue is nearly $700,000 in parish funds donated between 2004 and 2012 that have not been accounted for, the *Catholic News Reporter* pointed out.

On one charge, the government accuses Father Belczak of diverting more than $109,000 of parish funds to put a down payment on a condominium he purchased in 2005 from Verschuren. The FBI moved April 21, the day after Easter, to seize the condo.

The indictment also contends that Father Belczak spent money from a $420,000 bequest left by a parishioner who died in 2006 and intended the money to be used "for the needs of the church." According to the indictment, the priest deposited the funds in a money market account he kept secret from the archdiocese.

90

The government said Verschuren intercepted offering funds donated by parishioners on Mother's Day and Father's Day from 2007 through 2012. In addition, according to the indictment, she assisted Father Belczak in stealing more than $33,000 owed to the parish by Diocesan Publications and more than $26,000 in commissions paid to the parish's travel club.

While under suspension, Father Belczak continues to receive his salary from the archdiocese — which ranges from $27,500 to the mid $30,000s, plus benefits — and may perform priestly functions elsewhere in the archdiocese with prior approval. Recently, he has celebrated Masses at another suburban parish where his brother is the pastor, the *Catholic News Reporter* stated. The archdiocese, though, is not paying Father Belczak's legal costs.
*Reprinted in accordance with "fair use" guidelines.

Commentary: Belczak concealed the theft and diversion of nearly $500,000 by submitting false financial reports to the Archdiocese of Detroit. His reports understated the amount of the parish's operating receipts. The U.S. Attorney's Office, the FBI, and the Troy Police Department worked in concert to develop the charges in the indictment for mail fraud, wire fraud, and conspiracy.

While his lawyer tried to put a good face on the charges and supporters came to his defense, Belczak finally confessed, saying, "… I am at peace with all that has happened. Losing my job, home, and good reputation has brought me to my knees and here I found God waiting for me."

**

Catholic Priest Convicted of Stealing $130,000 from a Fund for the Poor*
December 15, 2014

Rev. Timothy Kane was found guilty of embezzling funds from the now-discontinued Angel Fund to help the poor of Detroit. Kane was also sentenced to pay $131,400 in restitution.

Father Timothy Kane of Detroit and his co-defendant, 34-year-old Dorreca Brewer of Jackson, were arraigned Wednesday. Prosecutors allege the pair scoured for needy families to apply for the money, and then took a large chunk of cash for themselves.

Father Kane, who has been a priest for 31 years, has worked at the Detroit Church of the Madonna and St. Gregory the Great — both in Detroit. He also acted as Christian Service Contactor at the Cathedral of the Most Blessed Sacrament.

A Wayne County Circuit Court jury found Kane guilty in October of six counts related to theft from the charity fund for poor people, including embezzlement between $1,000 and $20,000.

Kane, 58, testified that he didn't steal Angel Fund monies, even though he had signed a confession to police after his arrest in February. Kane said he signed the confession because of confusion related to his diabetes.

Kane was removed from the post, said Archdiocese of Detroit spokesman Joe Kohn. That is required under church law as an internal church legal proceeding takes place, said Kohn. He said he could not reveal the nature of the church inquiry taking place. The archdiocese did not pay for Kane's legal fees, said Kohn.

With imprisonment, "the salary would be ended," Kohn wrote in an e-mail. The archdiocese "does have an obligation to a priest of any status to provide 'basic support' financially... enough for room and board."
*Composite article based upon stories reported on 12/15/2014 in the *Detroit Free Press, Talking Points Memo.com*, and on WWJ Radio.

Commentary: Kane skimmed money for himself from the Angel Fund charity by conspiring with a state prison inmate who recruited people to make false requests for aid, which Kane then approved. Based on taped prison phone calls and his signed confession, Kane also had a sexual relationship with the inmate. However, Kane denied that relationship when he took the stand. Kane said he confessed because he was confused.

A woman, Dorreca Marvie Brewer of Jackson, was also part of the scheme. She was sentenced to five years of probation and fined $5,000 after a plea of no contest to similar charges.

The Angel Fund disbursed $17 million starting in 2005 from funds donated by an anonymous individual. The fund was designed to allow priests in Detroit churches to dispense aid quickly to people who needed help filling a prescription or making a mortgage payment. After Kane was charged, the Angel Fund donor discontinued operation.

***

The Fresno Bee
December 31, 2014

Tulare Priest Charged with Embezzlement*
By Hannah Furfaro

The former leader of St. Rita's Catholic Church in Tulare is being charged with embezzlement, officials from the Roman Catholic Diocese of Fresno announced Wednesday.

According to *The Fresno Bee,* the Tulare County District Attorney filed the charges against the Rev. Ignacio Villafan after being contacted by the diocese which discovered financial discrepancies under Villafan's watch, officials from the church say.

Villafan was removed from his position at St. Rita's in 2012 after the discrepancies were discovered. Teresa Dominguez, chancellor for the diocese, referred all questions about the case to the Tulare County DA's office. Officials did not immediately return phone messages.

***The Fresno Bee* indicated diocese officials said the church maintains an internal financial reporting and monitoring system to help detect financial misconduct. Clergy and staff are also trained to prevent fraud, officials said.**
*Reprinted in accordance with "fair use" guidelines.

Commentary: While officials maintained the Church had internal financial reporting and monitoring systems, Villafan was arrested for stealing $425,000. He wrote checks for his personal daily use — totaling more than $195,000 — and gave money from the Church to family members for their benefit. Presenting a tired, weak defense, his attorney stated, "I know the allegation is that he took so much from the Church; but I think what's been overlooked here is that he put much into the Church."

Interestingly, Bishop Armando Ochoa stated: "The breach of fiduciary responsibility of a pastor is more than just a monetary matter; it also carries with it a betrayal of a faith-based component where parishioners offer their support as a spiritual sacrifice, intended to support the missionary activity of the Church... therefore, this criminality is twofold, legal and relational."

CHAPTER TEN
Streams Increase and Debt Grows
2015

Unfunded pensions for priests surfaced as a major issue in 2015. In March (34), the *Boston Herald* reported the Archdiocese of Boston faced a financial crisis with a staggering $74M shortfall in their funding of pensions for their priests. At a funding level of 37 percent, they were well below the 65 percent classified as "critical" by the U.S. Department of Labor (if federal regulations had been applied).

Having closed churches and sold off property to solve other financial problems, the Archdiocese was now on a "pay-as-you-go basis," which expert Charles Zech said was a dangerous proposition.

On the other hand, Chicago's pension plan was funded above 90 percent. But, in accomplishing that goal, they had created huge funding liabilities for retirement benefits, such as medical coverage and housing. Expert consultant Jack Ruhl, from Western Michigan University, was quoted as saying, "Finances will be the next big scandal for the Church."

Later in the year, Reuters (36) reported that Catholic pension plans nationwide had a shortfall of $2B. Declining membership, dwindling donations, and rising expenditures resulted in 24 percent of the parishes in the country to run "red-ink" budgets in 2013.

In September, Patricia Lotich (28), founder of Smart Church Management, delineated eighteen facts about church embezzlement. Ten of her most cogent points follow:

- **An unbelievable 30 percent of all workers will steal.** If someone has a justified need, has easy access, and there are no controls, he/she is on a slippery slope to thievery.

- **An estimated 80 percent of church fraud cases don't get reported.** Most church fraud is handled behind the scenes, partly because of a desire to keep it private, the forgiving nature of people, and an inability to deal with internal strife.

- **Church thieves are creative.** They know how to take advantage of organizations with haphazard financial oversight, that doesn't enforce written policies or conduct audits.

- **Church leaders don't believe there's a crook amidst them.** A high level of faith and trust are a part of their personality; many are naïve and can't imagine a friend stealing.

- **Church theft often comes from the most trusted people.** Long-term employees know the system and the people in charge; they know the system and how to manipulate it.

- **An estimated 60 percent of churches don't have effective crime-prevention procedures in place.** They don't segregate functions or have adequate checks and balances.

- **Churches are targets for fraud because of their lax nature.** They are counterintuitive to suspecting someone of stealing and can't believe someone would steal from God.

- **One-third of all congregations fall victim to fraud.** Thievery doesn't occur because of chance or accident — it's by design because of the situation or people in control.

- **40 percent of frauds are caught through a tip.** Sometimes people talk too much, show off their gains through changes in their extravagant lifestyles, and get careless.

- **The average tenure of service for a thief is eight years.** While friendship and longevity are positive signs, they should not be confused with trustworthiness.

While the application of the percentages Lotich mentioned can be deceiving when applied to a small population, they are sobering when applied to any religious denomination.

The profile of the Catholic Church illustrates the point:

- **30 percent of all employees will steal.** The Catholic Church has over a million employees, the vast majority in hospitals and universities. Still, there are roughly 150,000 lay employees running the parishes and their schools (150,000 x .3 = 45,000).

- **An estimated 60 percent of churches don't have effective crime-prevention procedures in place.** There are 17,600 parishes in the country (17,600 x .6 = 10,560).

- **One third of all congregations fall victim to fraud.** Again, there are 17,600 parishes in the nation (17,600 x .33 = 5,808).

Point being, in translating the percentages to show the actual numbers — potential criminal activity is ever-present — church leaders must take advantage of policies, procedures, and resources available to prevent illegal actions.

***

The amount of dollars represented in notable cases increased slightly in 2015, coming to a total of $3,380,000. But the highlight of the year was NOT about the notable cases; it was about *the* notable case.

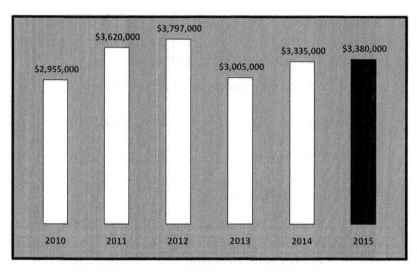

$2,955,000 $3,620,000 $3,797,000 $3,005,000 $3,335,000 $3,380,000

2010   2011   2012   2013   2014   2015

Chart 10 — Streams Grow and Debt Grows

In New York City, Father Peter Miqueli, the priest at St. Frances de Chantal in the Bronx, was alleged to have engaged in sexual and financial misconduct. The details of his alleged relationship with another man left little to the imagination and became an international story.

December 12, 2015
New York Post
Priest Accused of Paying His Sex 'Master' From Collection Plate Resigns

December 15, 2015
Daily Mail.com
Bronx 'Sex Slave' Priest Wants a Threesome with Him

December 16, 2015
The Tablet — International Catholic News Weekly — UK

New York Priest Accused of Stealing $1M to Pay for Gay Sex, Drugs, House, Steps Down

***

Gothamist
New York Public Radio
December 18, 2015

Priest Embezzled Church Money to Fund "Toilet Slave" S&M Lifestyle, Lawsuit Alleged*

According to the *Gothamist,* more sordid allegations have emerged from the lawsuit against Rev. Peter Miqueli, the Bronx priest accused of stealing over $1 million from two churches he worked at in order to finance his S&M lifestyle. *The New York Post* has obtained more emails sent to the church by Tatyana Gudin, the ex-girlfriend of Miqueli's alleged "master" Keith Crist, including one in which she explained their kinky relationship: "Keith has been Father Miqueli's gay, for-pay prostitute," she wrote in an email to Cardinal Timothy Dolan. "More specifically, Father Miqueli is Keith Crist's toilet slave."

The *Gothamist* reported that she helpfully explained exactly what a "toilet slave" is to the cardinal: "If you don't know what that means, Cardinal, I will break it down for you... Keith Crist uses Father Miqueli as his toilet, and Father Miqueli drinks his piss during their weekly, 3-day get-togethers when they take off to Father Miqueli's house in Brick, New Jersey, far away from prying eyes."

Among other accusations, Miqueli allegedly bought a $264,000 home in Brick, for himself and Crist, using embezzled money from the churches. Gudin gave more specific details to *The Post* about that house, which has a hot tub in the backyard and a statue of the Virgin Mary out front.

"Father Miqueli has a full-blown dungeon in the house," she wrote Dolan. "Master," she said Miqueli would e-mail Crist, "I can't wait to get to Jersey tonight, so I can drink your piss," the *Gothamist* said.

Gudin told *The Post*, "All the juicy stuff is what Keith would tell me face to face. We would be in bed together and he would say, 'Tatyana, I have to show you this.' I would be looking at those e-mails for sport."

"This one is my favorite," Gudin wrote the cardinal of the following e-mail: "Master, I don't really like drinking your piss, but I do it because I know it pleases you," the *Gothamist* pointed out.

Miqueli has been accused by a group of angry parishioners of siphoning off over $1 million since 2003 while leading St. Frances Xavier Cabrini on Roosevelt Island and St. Frances de Chantal in The Bronx. The lawsuit claims that Miqueli skimmed from collection plates, took money that had been donated to fix a church pipe organ, misappropriated funds from a church thrift shop, and more.

Miqueli allegedly used the money to pay for rough sex sessions with Crist, who was named as a co-defendant in the suit. In addition to the home in NJ, Miqueli also allegedly spent over $60,000 for "illicit and prescription drugs" he used with Crist, vacations in Italy and Florida, plus another $1,075.50 a month for Crist's East Harlem apartment. Gudin claims there was plenty of bad behavior at that apartment as well, the *Gothamist* reported.

"They would party. There would be needles and syringes all over the house," Gudin said. "There was equipment at the house — dildos, whips, chains, and chaps. Keith used it. The priest also used it," she said.

The sex toys, she said, were all bought by the priest. "This chastity belt was very unique," she told *The Post*. "It's also small, so when 'it' grows, you're in pain. I'm sure the priest buys all the equipment."

The ex-girlfriend also shared with Dolan that Miqueli wanted to have a threesome with her ("I, of course, declined"), and he had a sexual fantasy in which, "Keith [would take him] to Boro Park in Brooklyn, to the Hassidic section... to humiliate

him in public, in front of a pretty Jewish girl, the *Gothamist* reported.
*Reprinted in accordance with "fair use" guidelines.

Commentary: There's nothing more to add.

***

The Chippewa Herald
March 9, 2015

Eau Claire Woman Guilty of Bilking Former Priest of $317,884*
By Mike Tighe

According to *The Chippewa Herald,* an Eau Claire woman accused of preying on a former La Crosse Catholic priest's compassionate nature by bilking him out of $317,883.60 — at least part of it apparently for gambling sprees — faces up to 60 years in prison after pleading guilty to theft by false representation.

The Chippewa Herald indicated Cheri M. Hofkes-Zerwas, 54, had asked to plead no contest Friday to 23 felony counts of stealing more than $10,000 at a time from the Rev. John Schultz on numerous occasions.

Eau Claire County Assistant District Attorney Meri Larson spurned the possibility of a no-contest plea. Hofkes-Zerwas then consulted her attorney and agreed to plead guilty to six counts in the case, which was to have gone to a three-day trial Monday, as reported by *The Chippewa Herald.* The 17 other counts were dismissed but read into the record for possible consideration at her May 4 sentencing.
*Reprinted in accordance with "fair use" guidelines.

Commentary: Hofkes-Zerwas told the priest she needed extra dollars to keep her electricity from being shut off and to repay the Social Security Administration for benefit over-payments. Fact is, she had made 82 trips to Majestic Pines Casino in Black River Falls, with some excursions lasting days.

The scam surfaced when a corporate security officer for the bank, an Eau Claire police detective, reported that staffers at a local branch were concerned about large cash withdrawals made. In addition, she took nearly $51,000 in cash from her money market account. Fraud and financial exploitation increased in size and frequency over the 10-years.

***

WAVE 3 NEWS
August 17, 2015

Accountant Accused of Stealing $500K from Local Churches*

LOUISVILLE, KY (WAVE) — A woman at the center of a significant embezzlement investigation died before she could be charged, WAVE3.com has learned.

In a letter to parishioners from the Church of the Holy Spirit, the Rev Frederick Klotter wrote that LMPD investigators found the church's former business manager, Lisa Roth, embezzled more than $275,000 over several years.

WAVE3 News noted the Archdiocese of Louisville claimed she also stole $130,000 from St. Joseph and $110,000 from Holy Name.

That's when the Archdiocesan Finance Office discovered irregularities at the St. Joseph's and Holy Name parishes, where Roth worked after leaving Holy Spirit, WAVE3 News reported.

According to WAVE3 News, the Secret Service and Department of Justice also assisted in the investigation. They said she forged signatures, made checks out to herself, used the parish's credit cards, and quit before a random audit began.

Secret Service says Roth did not live an extravagant lifestyle, but rather spent some of the stolen money on daily living expenses.

"I was hurt and disappointed because you trust people," Father David Sanchez of St. Joseph told WAVE3 News. "I personally know the family, since they were little kids and I love them," he said of her children.

It's not clear how Roth died last month, at 60, but Klotter wrote that her survivors — including a husband of 27 years, knew nothing about her alleged crime.

"We seek to forgive and pray for those who have made mistakes," Klotter wrote.
*Reprinted according to "fair use" guidelines.

Commentary: Working as a long-term trusted employee, Roth functioned for the most part on her own, with limited supervision. There is no mention of any of the churches having a fully functioning financial committee.

In a letter to parishioners, Reverend Klotter wrote, "We seek to forgive and pray for those who have made mistakes."

***

The Wichita Eagle
September 1, 2015

Feds Charge Kansas Priest with Bank Fraud over Parish Thefts*

WICHITA — According to *The Wichita Eagle*, federal prosecutors charged a Kansas priest on Tuesday with stealing nearly $151,000 from two parishes and the Catholic Diocese of Wichita and using the money to fund his gambling.

Federal prosecutors alleged; documents filed in U.S. District Court in Wichita charge Father Thomas H. Leland with one count of bank fraud.

According to Diocese records, Leland was assigned to St. Francis Parish in St. Paul and St. Ambrose Parish in Erie, both located in southeast Kansas. "He is no longer active with the Diocese," spokeswoman Amy Pavlacka said.

"The charges filed today reflect a difficult time for the Catholic Diocese of Wichita," Pavlacka said in an email. "Our priorities throughout have been to assist and secure the financial well-being of St. Francis and St. Ambrose Catholic parishes, which we have done, and to help Fr. Leland navigate this difficult time with justice and mercy."
*Reprinted in accordance with the "fair use" guidelines.

Commentary: Leland, the only priest assigned to the parishes, had sole signature authority on each of the parishes' bank accounts. He took overpayments totaling $2,063 for conducting Mass, took unauthorized salary advances and salary overpayments totaling $138,200, and took unauthorized reimbursements for personal expenses totaling $10,656.

CHAPTER ELEVEN
Waters Flow
2016

By 2016 the impact of waves of thievery cases over the past few years had taken its toll. Fallout from sex abuse cases was no longer the sole scandal — the *thievery scandal* had taken its rightful place as one of the major issues facing the Church. Even use of the word *embezzlement* became commonplace in articles and news stories.

An influential document produced by the Center for Church Management & Business Ethics at Villanova University identified "Victimization by pattern of embezzlements," as one of the top five financial issues facing the Church.

Charles Zech, Director of the Villanova Center, was quoted in a *National Catholic Reporter* article by Peter Feuerherd (17) as saying, "The bishops are finally recognizing that embezzlement doesn't help their moral standing." Zech went on to note that attention was being given to "answering long-time critics, such as Michael W. Ryan, who has long argued that collection procedures in the parishes need tightening. He's been crying out in the desert."

(Since 2011, when Ryan (38) published *NONFEASANCE*, he's been critical of USCCB officials for shunning "the implementation of readily available, low-cost procedures that would virtually guarantee that every dollar placed in the collection plate is, in fact, deposited into the parish bank account.")

Feuerherd went on to provide numerous examples where efforts were underway to address parish collection security. He emphasized the importance of parishes taking action as an "estimated 40 percent of Sunday collections come from cash donations, seen as particularly vulnerable to pilfering."

In April, Brenden Canavan (7) tied the thievery and sex abuse issues together, referencing Pope Francis' efforts "to reinvigorate the Church's standing despite continuing corruption and abuse controversies."

Again, in November David Briggs (4) pointed to "the daunting financial issues challenging the Catholic Church" — from changing demographics to church embezzlement and the fallout from the clergy sex abuse scandal." He proceeded to raise questions about the wealthiest organization in the world — estimated at $170B. The Catholic Church had never been *under attack from so many forces.*

***

Full-fledged recognition of the ongoing *thievery scandal* was validated in 2016 with an increased flow of new cases. Across-the-board local newspapers, radio and TV stations, and online media outlets were filled with accounts of theft.

Smaller dollar-value cases were prominently displayed:

- The cafeteria manager at St. Albert the Greater Catholic Church of Kettering, Ohio reportedly wrote checks and made debit card purchases of approximately $45,000 from the Church's cafeteria account.

- A Seymour, Indiana priest was arrested for embezzling $20,000 from the Church.

- A woman was sentenced for 18 months in a church embezzlement case in Choctaw, Oklahoma, $500,000 missing,

- The treasurer for the business arm of KOC, affiliated with St. Michael's Catholic Church of Port Richey, Florida, was charged with stealing $80,000.

- A Pennsylvania Township woman pleaded guilty to a church theft case of $46,000; an internal audit revealed more than $82,000 was missing.

- A former priest was accused of stealing $76,000 from a Leonardtown, Maryland church.

- An Austin, Texas woman was placed on probation for a $40,000 church theft.

***

The slow growth in notable cases occurring from 2013 accelerated in 2016, increasing by nearly $600,000.

At the top of the range, it was more of the same — another priest gained national attention. It happened in Huber Heights (Dayton area), Ohio, where a priest was convicted of stealing nearly $2M.

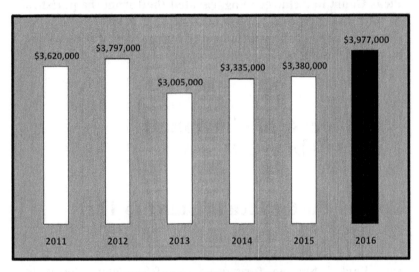

Chart 11 — Waters Flow

***

The Catholic Telegraph
(Cincinnati)
March 10, 2016

Father Simone Pleads Guilty to Theft, Plea Deal includes Jail Time*

A former pastor of St. Peter Church in Huber Heights pleaded guilty Thursday, March 10 in Montgomery County Pleas Court to a charge of aggravated theft from the parish... in part the plea deal... stipulated Father Simone will serve five years of jail time with no early release, and will repay the parish $1.9 million.

***

Archdiocese of Cincinnati
FOR IMMEDIATE RELEASE
March 10, 2016

Former Pastor Pleads Guilty to Theft Charge*

Rev. Earl F. Simone, former pastor of St. Peter Church in Huber Heights, today pleaded guilty in Montgomery County Common Pleas Court to a charge of aggravated theft from the parish.

"Service to the people of God as a pastor is a sacred trust," said Most Reverend Dennis M. Schnurr, Archbishop of Cincinnati. "Fr. Simone's violation of that trust has saddened and deeply disappointed me.

"When Archdiocesan staff members and I have visited St. Peter, we have been impressed by the vibrancy of the parish and school. Our staff will do all that they can to help the parish move forward under the leadership of the current pastor, Rev. Anthony Cutcher, while continuing to pray for healing in the parish."

Fr. Simone, 75, ceased serving the parish in March 2015 and officially resigned as pastor of St. Peter and three other parishes in April. He also retired from active ministry at the same time. He does not receive a pension from the Archdiocese because he receives a full military pension from his prior service as an officer.

Officials of the Archdiocese received an ethics complaint regarding financial misconduct at St. Peter on Feb. 11, 2015. After a brief internal investigation, the Archdiocese reported the allegations to the local law enforcement authorities and retained an outside auditing firm with expertise in forensic accounting, as outlined in a March 18, 2015 press release.

Through the remainder of 2015, a forensic accounting firm hired by the Archdiocese, an outside insurance consultant, and Archdiocesan auditing staff worked through bank records, credit card transactions, vendor invoices, and other financial records going back many years to determine the extent of the irregularities. The Archdiocese regularly met with representatives of the Huber Heights Police Department and the Montgomery County Prosecutor's Office.

*Reprinted from a public news release.

Commentary: The difference between the language of the news story summarized above and the news release from the Archdiocese is dramatic — one presents facts and the other presents process. At first impression, the news release from the Archdiocese seems to provide a sense of openness and transparency, but in fact, its descriptive nature provides little information about the case.

Simone also faced a $4 million lawsuit filed by the archdiocese, which alleged that he stole far more than he admitted, and had up to 10 non-clerical, unnamed co-conspirators who assisted him in stealing church funds.

"Simone has repaid nothing, but St. Peter will receive $3M from the archdiocese and their insurance company," the prosecuting attorney said.

Archbishop Schnurr's reaction to this entire situation is one of great sadness. He pointed out that while Pope Francis had declared 2016 The Year of Mercy, "there's mercy but there is also justice. When somebody commits a crime or makes a mistake, they must pay the price."

***

Department of Justice
U.S. Attorney's Office
Western District of Kentucky
September 6, 2016

Louisville Attorney Sentenced To 48 Months*

> *Ordered to pay $1,602,327.14 to multiple victims including $268,459.06 to St. Mary's Church and $245,993.67 to WHAS Crusade for Children*

LOUISVILLE, KY – United States Attorney John E. Kuhn, Jr. announced today that David Cary Ford, 54, of Louisville, Kentucky, was sentenced to 48 months in federal prison following his conviction on criminal counts of wire fraud and money laundering stemming from Ford's actions while he was a practicing attorney and the executor of seven estates in Louisville.

"Attorneys are professionally and ethically bound to serve their clients' best interests," stated U.S. Attorney John Kuhn. "We simply cannot tolerate attorneys or any other fiduciaries using their positions of trust to steal from those they are obligated to protect. This prosecution serves the principle of justice and vindicates the breach of a trust that is an essential component of a multitude of professional relationships."

As part of his sentence, Ford was ordered to pay over $1.6 million in restitution to 21 different victims who would have received that amount, according to bequests in the wills written by the individuals whose estates were defrauded, if not for Ford's fraud. Those victims and the restitution they are owed include $245,993.67 that would have gone to the WHAS Crusade for Children and $5,598.59 for the Little Sisters of the Poor.

110

Local victims included St. Mary's Church ($268,459.06), St. Francis of Assisi Church ($44,743.18), Holy Family Catholic Church ($2,799.30), Our Mother of Sorrows Catholic Church ($2,799.30), and the Archdiocese of Louisville ($89,486.35).

Other victims included the Passionist Nuns ($245,993.67), the National Shrine of St. Elizabeth Ann Seton ($134,229.53), the Franciscan Sisters of Allegany, Inc. ($134,229.53), the Catholic Foreign Mission Society of America, Inc. ($44,743.18), and the Sisters of Charity of St. Joseph's ($44,743.18).

*Reprinted from a public news release.

Commentary: There is a natural level of trust people have for their legal counsel, and rightfully so. However, the details of this case illustrate how the "faith-based" philosophy of these organizations and their leaders opened the door to people like Mr. Ford. And, he took advantage of it.

***

WPXI.COM
May 27, 2016

Police: Religious Brother Accused of Stealing $220K from Church had a Gambling Problem*

AMBRIDGE, PA — According to WPXI.com, a religious brother is facing criminal charges for allegedly stealing more than $220,000 in parish funds from a church in Ambridge, Beaver County.

Thomas Ross, otherwise known as Brother Ambrose, is accused of stealing the money from Good Samaritan Parish between 2006 and 2015, according to the Beaver County District Attorney.

Parish officials noticed missing funds in early 2015, prompting an investigation by the Ambridge Police

Department, auditors from the Diocese of Pittsburgh, and the Pennsylvania State Police.

A release from the Beaver County District Attorney said that surveillance equipment was installed in parish offices in April 2015 and Ross was recorded taking sealed bank envelopes from a secured cabinet on four occasions.

When Ross was confronted about the video and missing funds in May 2015, he admitted to the theft, the release said.

"He was astonished himself... about the amount. He didn't even have the amount; how much it was. He was astonished when he found out how much it was," Ambridge police Chief Jim Mann said.

WPIX.com indicated a Pittsburgh diocese forensic audit revealed more than $24,000 missing from loose weekly collections from 2012 to 2015, more than $141,000 missing from parishioner envelope contributions from 2012 to 2015, and more than $54,000 missing from votive candle contributions from 2006 to 2015.

*Reprinted in accordance with "fair use" guidelines.

Commentary: Ross had a severe gambling problem; his Players Card account with the River Casino in Pittsburgh recorded gambling transactions of nearly $3M. During the time in which he was under investigation (knowing that he was going to be arrested), he continued to gamble at the casino. He was charged with three third-degree felonies of theft by unlawful taking, two third-degree felonies of receiving stolen property, and one third-degree misdemeanor of receiving stolen property.

***

Florida Today

September 6, 2016

Police: Rockledge Priest Facing Fraud Lived Above Means*

By J.D. Gallup

Police say a Rockledge priest took widow's money, spent thousands on everything from car payments to gourmet chocolate.

It began with a simple question from a widow about her bank account and ended with Rockledge detectives and Orlando Diocese accountants poring over financial statements and looking into the spending habits of a longtime priest, 73-year-old Father Nicholas King.

What detectives say they uncovered, according to court documents, was a priest who funneled money into his own private account with expenses that ranged from several hundred dollars in restaurant meals, a $9,000 down payment on a car, $6,000 to his sister, and $700 in spending at a gourmet chocolate shop.

Last week, Father King of St. Mary's Catholic Church in Rockledge, was arrested on charges of grand theft from a person older than 65 years of age, in excess of $50,000, and organized fraud involving funds over $50,000, records show. No court date has been set.

Rockledge police began investigating the case August 24 after a 79-year-old widow notified church authorities that her money market account set aside for assisting the church was overdrawn, records show. Police said King was "surprised" by the investigation and denied any wrongdoing.

"(King) has been active at that church for 20-plus years," said Donna Seyferth, spokeswoman for the Rockledge Police Department. She said the widow's concerns were reported to police by the Orlando Diocese.

Seyferth said that detectives found that the 73-year-old priest, whose three residences included the rectory provided by the church and a Cocoa Beach condo, was living far above his annual $28,000 salary.

"He said if there were any discrepancies it would need to be addressed with the church's bookkeeper," Seyferth said.

Detectives also uncovered potential evidence of other financial concerns at the church when it was learned that King had apparently used the widow's money to help cover payroll for the church's Catholic school.

Police said the diocese was also conducting its own accounting investigation into the handling of the congregation's finances.
*Reprinted with permission from *Florida Today.*

Commentary: Detectives sorted through canceled checks, financial records, and bank statements belonging to the widowed parishioner. The woman's late husband originally set up the money market trust account to support the Church. The woman pointed out that the account — which at one point held over $100,000 — was overdrawn.

The investigation proved a swift change of fortune for King, who celebrated his 50th year of service in the Church earlier in the year. He was released from the Brevard County Jail Complex after his $87,000 bond was posted.

***

Post Bulletin
September 30, 2016

Woman Accused of Stealing $200,000 from Church Gets 10 days in Jail*
By Kay Fate

ALBERT LEA, MN — According to the *Post Bulletin*, a church bookkeeper accused of stealing nearly $200,000 from an Albert Lea church and its affiliated school was sentenced Thursday to 10 days in jail and placed on probation for 20 years.

Ryan Mae McFarland, formerly known as Ryan Mae Schoppe, 37, pleaded guilty in July in Freeborn County District Court to two counts of felony theft by swindle. In exchange for the plea, seven identical counts were dismissed, said the *Post Bulletin*.

McFarland, an Austin resident, was also ordered to complete 100 hours of community work service; a restitution hearing has been set for December. The money she's accused of taking has all been spent, court documents show.

The investigation began March 11, 2015 when Albert Lea police were contacted by officials at St. Theodore Catholic Church after an audit by the financial office of the Diocese of Winona.

Based on records kept by the church and St. Theodore's School, it appeared money received as offerings, donations, and fees had been stolen from the facilities' bank accounts.

The money had been taken by McFarland between August 2013 and February 2015, the criminal complaint says, during her time as bookkeeper for the two facilities.

The total amount misappropriated by McFarland, per the audit of all financial records, is $199,771.29.

*Reprinted with approval to use a representative excerpt following "fair use" guidelines, per the *Post Bulletin*.

Commentary: McFarland did it all. She was responsible for payroll and benefits, overseeing contributions and the money counters of the weekly collections, handling tax information, and providing information to the Church administrator for the purpose of budgeting.

Because she worked in essentially a control-free environment, she regularly paid herself extra money and made bogus entries about what the money was for. Nearly $53,000 was misappropriated through her false payroll records.

She used church funds to pay off a 2012 civil judgment against her.

CHAPTER TWELVE
Troubled Waters
2017

In a timely January article, "How to stop embezzlement in your parish," Charles Zech (50) reminded readers of his research findings of 2007, that 85 percent of dioceses experience embezzlement, and it had not subsided in the last decade. "Catholic dioceses and parishes are notoriously careless with their internal financial controls. The bottom line is that they're simply too trusting."

While Zech had earlier produced volumes of materials for bishops, priests, and parishioners to use to ensure sound financial procedures, he acknowledged ten years later, "The problem has not subsided." The percentage of parishes without committee supervision had dropped to 7 percent; still, when applied to the 17,651 parishes at the time, over 1,200 parishes were at "total" risk.

While many parishes were at risk, Bob Smietana (41) reminded readers that the Catholic Church is not the only faith group that collects billions of dollars per year, and not all of it ends up where it's supposed to go. "About one in 10 Protestant churches has someone embezzle funds, according to a survey of 1,000 Protestant senior pastors."

In a much earlier study, Herbert Lowe (28) found about one in five of all Catholic churches have had someone embezzle funds. Definitive conclusions cannot be drawn from the data in different studies and different time frames. However, it's reasonable to assume thievery in Catholic churches occurs much more frequently than in their Protestant counterparts.

A noteworthy international event occurred in June of 2017. Sixty-nine priests in Indonesia resigned after accusing their bishop of embezzlement. They suggested he secretly borrowed over $124,000 from some of the accounts without providing an accountability report. With suspicions, the money had gone to a woman with whom the bishop was rumored to be having an affair. He was alleged to have said it was none of their business. While it was an international event, it rang a bell loud and clear throughout Indonesia's dioceses and parishes — perhaps bishops worldwide were no longer untouchable!

***

The dollar amount of notable cases skyrocketed in 2017, jumping more than $2.3M to a total of $6,240,000. Leading the way were cases of $1.4M and $2M, followed by additional events totaling $832,000 and $535,000.

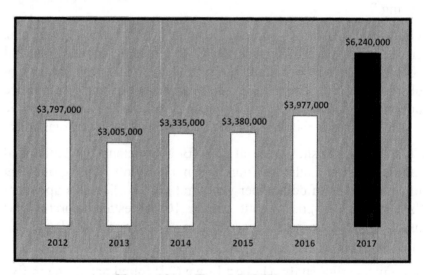

Chart 12 — Troubled Waters

***

Akron Beacon Journal/Ohio.com

March 1, 2017

Late Priest Accused of Stealing $160,000 from Streetsboro Parish*

According to the *Akron Beacon Journal,* a beloved Catholic priest who died unexpectedly last year has been accused of stealing about $160,000 from the St. Joan of Arc parish in Streetsboro.

The *Beacon Journal* indicated the money was discovered missing after the Rev. Pat Ferraro, 51, died Sept. 2 of a heart attack.

The Catholic Diocese of Youngstown alerted parishioners over the weekend about the missing funds and Streetsboro police are investigating.

Police Chief Darin Powers said much of the investigative work already has been done by the diocese.

Police are now verifying the financial numbers and trying to determine if anyone else was involved.

Powers declined to say what happened to the money.

The *Beacon Journal* indicated an independent auditing firm was then hired to conduct a full audit of parish finances and discovered that Ferraro took about $160,000 over a period of four years for his personal use.

The diocese said it has instituted a new policy of rotating financial audits at all parishes and institutions and is increasing the frequency of workshops to educate parish financial council members on their role in overseeing parish finances.

Ferraro was popular and well-respected in the Streetsboro community and "served the parish in a remarkable way," said Monsignor John Zuraw, the diocesan chancellor.

*Reprinted in accordance with "fair use" guidelines.

Commentary: While diocese and parish officials indicated appropriate procedures were in place, two complaints from outside the structure were received about "financial irregularities" at the parish. The diocese then initiated an investigation that confirmed problems, and wisely hired an outside accounting firm.

***

CatholicPhilly.com
April 6, 2017

Priest Charged with Stealing $500K from Fund for Clergy Retirement Home*
By Matthew Gambino

A priest of the Archdiocese of Philadelphia responsible for a retirement home for priests faces federal charges of embezzling more than $535,000 from that same home.

Msgr. William A. Dombrow, 77, was charged by the U.S. District Attorney in Philadelphia on April 5 with four counts of wire fraud in a scheme he is alleged to have devised to siphon off funds intended for the care of retired archdiocesan priests at Villa St. Joseph, Darby, where he has served as the rector since 2005.

Catholic Human Services of the archdiocese operates the nursing care and residence for 50 retired and ill archdiocesan priests.

The District Attorney alleges that Msgr. Dombrow set up an account at Sharon Savings Bank in Darby unbeknownst to the archdiocese, directed money from the estates of retired or deceased priests as well as bequests of lay donors to Villa St. Joseph, and transferred money electronically for his personal use.

The scheme is alleged to have begun in December 2007 and continued through May 2016. In a statement, the District Attorney charges that the priest "had sole access" to the bank account, "which was funded by gifts from wills and life insurance proceeds that were intended for the archdiocese."

The District Attorney's office expects Msgr. Dombrow to plead guilty to the charges by the end of April. If convicted on all charges, he faces a maximum of 80 years in jail plus fines, and three years of supervised release.

*Reprinted from a public website, per *CatholicPhilly.com.*

Commentary: Msgr. Dombrow was ordained in 1970 by the Archdiocese of Philadelphia and was very active in various archdiocese committees. Serving as rector for an archdiocese-operated retirement home for priests, he siphoned off funds for his personal use, which funded his frequent visits to Harrah's Casino in Chester. His scheme went on for nine years before bank officials became suspicious and notified the archdiocese.

***

MLive.com
FLINT
September 22, 2017

Retired Priest Gets Prison Time, Must Repay Church in Embezzlement Case*
By Dominic Adams

CORUNNA, MI — A former priest was sentenced to at least five years in prison and must pay $127,000 in restitution after admitting to embezzling tens of thousands of dollars from an Owosso church.

The Rev. David Ernest Fisher was sentenced on Friday, Sept. 22, to five to 15-years in prison, must pay $127,000 in restitution, and another $992 in fines and court costs, according to the Shiawassee County Clerk's Office.

Fisher oversaw St. Joseph Catholic Church in Owosso for 23 years and retired to North Dakota in June 2015. Suspicion arose when the church's new pastor noticed some figures were off with the parish's finances, according to officials with the Catholic Diocese of Lansing.

*Reprinted with permission of MLive.com and Barcroft Studios.

Commentary: In Michigan, investigations into suspected thefts can only go back six years due to the statute of limitations. The audit revealed more than $450,000 was missing. Fisher was charged with one count of embezzlement of over $100,000. The Church secretary was also charged with one count of embezzlement from a charitable organization.

***

The Post
Royaltonpost.com
June 3, 2017

Royalton Resident Sentenced for Embezzling from Catholic Charities*

The former business manager and comptroller for Cleveland Catholic Charities was sentenced to more than five years in prison for embezzling $2 million from the organization, said Acting U.S. Attorney David A. Sierleja and Stephen D. Anthony, special agent in charge of the FBI's Cleveland Office.

Michelle Medrick, 58, of North Royalton, previously pleaded guilty to bank fraud. U.S. District Judge Christopher Boyko sentenced Medrick to 62 months in federal prison and ordered her to pay $2.4 million in restitution.

Medrick embezzled $2 million from Catholic Charities of the Diocese of Cleveland beginning in at least 2008 through last year.

She was employed as the comptroller and the business manager for Catholic Charities at Parmadale, a facility that provides a variety of services in Parma. She was responsible for payroll, accounts payable, accounts receivable, and other financial transactions.

"This defendant stole millions of dollars from the vulnerable men, women and children who are supported by the good works of Catholic Charities," Sierleja said. "The Diocese uncovered the fraud, came forward to federal authorities and cooperated fully."

*Reprinted from a public news release, per *The Post*.

Commentary: As the comptroller and business manager, Medrick had unlimited control over accounts payable and receivable. She converted client-agency and donor checks to cash, which she then deposited to her own bank account. She wrote more than 1,400 checks payable to cash and misrepresented herself as the agency's chief financial officer so she could withdraw cash from the Catholic Charities' bank accounts.

***

Retired Priest Charged with Stealing from Canton Parish*
December 31, 2017

A longtime Archdiocese of Detroit priest has been ordered to stand trial on charges of stealing money and property from the church.

The Rev. Eugene Katcher, 71, former pastor at Resurrection Parish in Canton Township, was arraigned in Plymouth's 35th District court on three counts of larceny and could face up to four years in prison if he is convicted in Wayne County Circuit Court.

The charges stem from allegations he stole money from the collection plate, votive candle donations, and other donations parishioners made to the church. Katcher, banned from his former church, came under investigation last spring after the Archdiocese of Detroit was made aware of potential wrongdoing, the Archdiocese has said.

After uncovering evidence of possible improper activity, the Archdiocese contacted civil authorities, the news release stated. The alleged crimes occurred from February 2016 to July 15, 2017, said Maria Miller, spokeswoman for the Wayne County Prosecutor's Office. In addition to the money, Katcher allegedly stole several items from the church, including a television and bottles of wine.

Katcher voluntarily waived his right to a preliminary examination and has been released on a personal bond. The amount of money Katcher is accused of taking hasn't been divulged, though authorities say the crimes occurred from early 2016 until July of this year.

In its news release, the Archdiocese said it "takes seriously every allegation involving inappropriate conduct of clergy, church personnel or volunteers." Moreover, the Archdiocese conducts a financial audit of parishes every three years and each parish must have a parishioner-led finance council to advise the pastor on oversight and control of parish financial affairs.

*Composite article based upon stories reported in the 9/20/17 issue of the *Hometown Life* and the 8/31/17 issues of *The Detroit News* and *Detroit Free Press*.

Commentary: Reverend Katcher was accused of stealing from the collection plate and stealing numerous pieces of church property. The amount of theft was not disclosed. While judges and cases are different, the possibility of four years in prison suggests misappropriations in the range of $200,000.

After uncovering the financial misconduct, the Archdiocese contacted civil authorities.

***

The Mercury News
October 3, 2017

San Jose: Catholic Priest Sentenced for Embezzling $1.4 Million*
By Jason Green

Court document say Hien Mink Nguyen believed he could make better use of funds for his parishioners.

SAN JOSE, CA — As a priest for the Diocese of San Jose, 57-year-old Hien Mink Nguyen funneled more than $1.4 million in church donations into his bank accounts over a five-year period, but the princely sum sat mostly untouched, according to court records.

Tensions that Nguyen believed existed between the Vietnamese Catholic community in San Jose and the Diocese reportedly were what drove his criminal conduct. He believed that he could make better use of the money for parishioners than the Diocese.

"How else can we explain why he failed to spend a dime of the money and leave it all as deposits in his own bank accounts," Nguyen's San Francisco-based attorney, Jay R. Weill, wrote in a September 27 sentencing memorandum.

Whatever his motivations were, Nguyen now faces time behind bars. On Tuesday, a U.S. District Court judge ordered him to serve three years in prison, followed by three years of supervised release. He also was ordered to pay back the embezzled money.

Nguyen, a refugee of the Vietnam War, deposited checks made payable to the center into his bank accounts. He also stole cash donations as a priest at Saint Patrick Cathedral.

Federal authorities entered the picture in 2012, and by December 1, 2015, a grand jury had issued a superseding indictment charging Nguyen with 14 counts of bank fraud and four counts of tax evasion. Nguyen ultimately pleaded guilty to the tax evasion charges in August 2016 and was convicted of bank fraud charges.

*Reprinted with the permission of *The Mercury News*.

Commentary: Anonymous complaints sparked an investigation by the diocese, which found Nguyen had written more than $30,000 worth of checks against the Church's bank accounts to cover personal expenses. He agreed to repay the funds but kept secret the fact he'd stolen more than $1.4M.

A continuing probe uncovered the remaining amount, which Nguyen had placed in a separate account. Because the embezzled funds sat largely untouched in his bank account, Nguyen was able to fully repay the diocese. His lawyer said his client plans to use the $500,000 he posted as bail when he was arrested in 2015 to pay the IRS.

***

United States Department of Justice
UNITED STATES ATTORNEY'S OFFICE
WESTERN DISTRICT OF WISCONSIN
November 9, 2017

West Salem Woman Sentenced to 4 Years for Wire Fraud & Tax Evasion*

MADISON, WIS. -- Jeffrey M. Anderson, Acting United States Attorney for the Western District of Wisconsin, announced that Barbara Snyder, 59, West Salem, Wisconsin, was sentenced today by U.S. District Judge James D. Peterson to four years in federal prison for engaging in a wire fraud scheme and filing a false income tax return. Snyder pleaded guilty to these charges on August 25, 2017.

Snyder served as the secretary and accounting clerk for St. Patrick's Church in Onalaska, Wisconsin. Between 2006 and 2015, Snyder embezzled approximately $832,210 of church collections. Although she was entrusted to deposit all of the church collections, Snyder took a portion of the funds for herself.

Judge Peterson sentenced Snyder to a four-year period of imprisonment on the wire fraud charge and a concurrent 12-month period of imprisonment on the tax charge. Judge Peterson admonished Snyder for concealing her conduct and engaging in a scheme that had a dramatic impact on the church and community.

*Reprinted from a public news release.

Commentary: To avoid detection, Snyder discarded records from the Church collections, created false entries in accounting records, and lied to church auditors. At the same time, Snyder filed a false Individual Income Tax Return for 2015, in which she underreported her gross income by failing to report the proceeds of her embezzlement, which she used to feed her gambling problem.

CHAPTER THIRTEEN
The Hundred-Year Flood
2018

With the number and size of embezzlement cases on the rise, articles and books flooded the literary market — guides to follow, tips to prevent, how to stop — all constructive and well intended! Unfortunately, hundreds in the Church failed to heed the message.

In "Protecting God's Money:...," Rob Forney (18) defined three salient points for all to consider. He described the 'Fraud Triangle' and pointed out critical conditions that enhance the possibility of fraud occurring:

- **Perceived Pressure:** Coming from financial instability — family, career, ambition, or internal greed.

- **Rationalization:** An individual justifies a fraudulent act — feels he/she is deserving, can spend the money more wisely, or has a greater need.

- **Opportunity:** There are poor controls, lack of accountability, or a laissez-faire environment is present.

- He also indicated the ACFE 2018 Report to the Nations found that 89 percent of perpetrators studied had never been charged or convicted of anything, and concluded, "Fraud prevention is an ongoing process; parishes of any size could become victims."

- Good advice, as the number of less-dollar-value cases, as illustrated below, continued to escalate:

- A Johnson County (Kansas) priest charged with two counts of computer crime was accused of stealing $42,000.

- A church administrator from Tuscola County (Michigan) was accused of embezzling thousands of dollars.

- A former bookkeeper at St. Joseph Catholic Church in Kingston (New York) was indicted on 63 counts for stealing $68,000.

- A former deacon and business manager at St. Joan of Arc Catholic Church in St. Clair Shores (Michigan) charged with stealing was sentenced to probation for embezzlement.

- A former Assistant Superintendent of a Catholic School in Washington (D.C.) was arrested and charged with embezzling $45,000.

- A volunteer was sentenced to five years of probation for stealing over $35,000 from a charitable gaming fund at St. Pius X Catholic Church in Burton (Michigan).

***

Notable cases continued their trajectory, with another $1.7M increase, topping out in 2018 at $7,932,000 — more than doubling the amount just two years before.

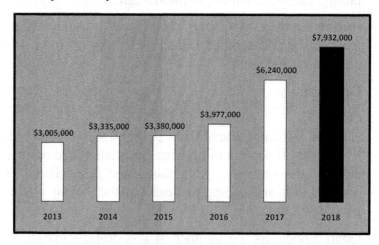

Chart 13 — The Hundred-Year Flood

The year wasn't exceptional due to the record-setting to amount; rather, once again, there was a case that grabbed the attention with its scope.

National Catholic Reporter
Trial Pending for Priest Accused of Embezzling $5 Million from Parish

USA TODAY NETWORK
Lawsuit Accuses Michigan Priest of Spending Embezzled Funds on Lavish Estate

***

Lansing State Journal
June 28, 2018

After $5M Embezzlement, How a Michigan Catholic Community Rebounded*
By Christopher Haxel

With trial looming, St. Martha parish powers forward

OKEMOS — In 2014, Tom and Sharon O'Dea were new to Lansing and looking for a Roman Catholic parish to join. They attended mass at a few local churches, but ultimately settled on St. Martha — a small parish with a big church.

That church, with its soaring ceiling and walls of stained-glass windows, was impressive, Tom O'Dea said. But it was the people who drew them in. "They were more friendly," he said. "We felt closer to them, felt we had more in common with them than we did with people at other parishes."

The Rev. Jonathan Wehrle, who founded the parish in 1988, "wasn't a real warm person... wasn't an easy person to get close to," Tom O'Dea said, "and that kind of bothered us. But we thought, 'That's not what we're here for. We're here for our religion and for the people.'"

Wehrle was a good priest who gave excellent homilies, Tom said, but the couple found it strange that Wehrle was the only priest around. Every other parish they'd belonged to had at least one priest or deacon to assist the pastor.

And looking back, O'Dea, 75, also remembers something strange about how Wehrle handled collections: "He had this big, great big, wooden box. After mass, he'd walk down the aisle with that box. And I'd think to myself, 'Geez, oh man, how can they let that be?'"

Rev. Jonathan Wehrle appears in district court for his preliminary hearing on embezzlement charges in Judge Donald Allen, Jr.'s courtroom Friday, Sept. 1, 2017. Wehrle is the founding pastor of St. Martha Parish in Okemos.

O'Dea had served as an usher before, and at other churches the cash and checks donated from parishioners were quickly counted and locked up by a rotating cast of volunteers.

"(Wehrle) walked out of there like, 'Here's my money,'" O'Dea said.

Now, while Wehrle awaits trial more than a year after his arrest on felony embezzlement charges after allegedly stealing more than $5 million from the parish, St. Martha is still recovering from the shock.

*Reprinted with permission of the *Lansing State Journal*.

Commentary: Detailed comment provided in the next chapter.

***

Port Aransas — South Jetty
July 5, 2018

Church Members Angered Over Arrest of Priest*
By Zack Perkins

Some parishioners of St. Joseph Catholic Church in Port Aransas (TX) are expressing outrage over the arrest of the church's former priest, the Rev. Kris Bauta.

Bauta has been accused of stealing more than $150,000 from the Roman Catholic Diocese of Corpus Christi.

Mike Fawdry, a North Padre Island resident who had attended St. Joseph since 2013, said he doesn't believe Bauta committed the crime.

"The whole thing is just a travesty," he said.

Bauta was at the center of a controversy when he said that the diocese dismissed him from his Port Aransas post with no explanation in October. He had been the priest at St. Joseph for more than four years.

Bauta was arrested on Tuesday, June 26, on a second-degree felony theft charge, according to Sgt. Nathan Brandley, a spokesman for the Texas Rangers. The priest was released on $50,000 bond on Wednesday, June 27.

The diocese said in a news release that Bauta was removed from St. Joseph after a "financial audit revealed severe irregularities." The release wasn't more specific about the alleged irregularities and mentioned nothing about donated Hurricane Harvey funds.

After becoming aware of the irregularities, the diocese turned the matter over to officers with the Texas Rangers who have been investigating Bauta for "several months," the release said.

An affidavit for an arrest warrant says Bauta was arrested for allegedly stealing more than $150,000 from the diocese, according to court records.

"I am in shock and devastated with the viciousness of the accusations," Bauta said in the statement. "God knows that I am innocent. His justice and truth will prevail. I would like to thank the hundreds of people from Port Aransas and beyond for standing by me in my trials."
*Reprinted with permission of the *Port Aransas South Jetty.*

Commentary: Credit card statements showed Bauta had purchased items that were refunded by the diocese. Once he was refunded the money, he would return the items, depositing the funds in his account.

***

The Christian Post
July 5, 2018

Woman Faces 20 Years in Prison for Embezzling Over $800K from Her Church*

According to *The Christian Post*, a 63-year-old woman has been found guilty of embezzling more than $818,000 from a Catholic church in Wisconsin.

Deborah Marcellus, who served as the director of development of St. Joseph's Catholic Church in Rice Lake, this week pleaded guilty in U.S. District Court in Madison to wire fraud and filing a false income tax return, according to the Sawyer County Record.

Marcellus generated more than 200 fraudulent checks from church bank accounts for $818,604 from 2011 until April 2017, according to an investigation done by the IRS and the Rice Lake Police Department. St. Joseph's Church and the Diocese of Superior cooperated in the probe, *The Christian Post* said.

Court records indicate U.S. District Judge James Peterson has scheduled sentencing for Oct. 2, and she faces up to 20 years in federal prison.
Reprinted in accordance with "fair use" guidelines.

Commentary: The congregation trusted Marcellus so much; she was the only one who handled the Church's money. Additionally, she led church leaders to believe that the Church would have to close due to financial woes, which was also part of her scam.

She used computer software to generate checks to herself from multiple bank accounts belonging to the Church. After depositing the checks, she used the money for a large variety of personal expenses, including excessive gambling. During the same time, she filed false income tax returns, thereby, underreporting her gross income.

***

Sun Sentinel

August 19, 2018

Pompano Beach Priest Resigns After Church Says He Stole More Than $200K*

By Aric Chokley

Father Henryk Pawelec, of St. Coleman's Catholic Church in Pompano Beach, resigned as pastor at St. Coleman's Catholic Church after the Archdiocese of Miami said he stole money from the church "for his personal benefit."

A Pompano Beach church held Mass Sunday, but without its pastor.

Pawelec also paid back $236,469 to the church and could face legal action after the parish reported the incident to the State Attorney's Office, the Archdiocese said Sunday.

"This breach of trust on the part of Father Pawelec, I am sure, deeply saddens and disappoints you as much as it saddens and disappoints me," Miami Archbishop Thomas Wenski said in a statement.

The Archdiocese received reports that Pawelec was diverting money and reviewed the congregation's financial records. Pawelec agreed to resign Wednesday.

*Reprinted with permission from the *Sun Sentinel*.

Commentary: Archbishop Wenski said it all when he wrote, "Father (Pawelec) could only have diverted these funds because he, as pastor, deliberately chose to ignore Archdiocesan policies on the proper handling of parish funds." However, these same policies and the accounting controls were in place, allowing others to determine the amount of funds pocketed by the priest, which he gave back.

***

KMBC 9NEWS

August 22, 2018

Blue Springs Church Wants Justice and Forgiveness After Clerk Steals Nearly $450K*

The clerk had worshiped and worked at the church for more than 30 years.

BLUE SPRINGS, MO — According to *KMBC 9News,* police are investigating after a church in Blue Springs says a clerk stole nearly $450,000. The Diocese of Kansas City-St. Joseph says the longtime clerk admitted to the theft. Now the church wants justice, and forgiveness.

Forgiveness isn't always easy. "It's a huge amount of money," said Father John Bolderson.

KMBC 9News indicated that Bolderson, St. Robert Bellarmine Parish, and its congregation are trying. Weeks ago, the church's finance council was struggling to rectify its checks. Bolderson asked his clerk about the missing money.

"She said, 'I took them... I took them,'" Bolderson said. That's when the path to forgiveness, and criminal charges, began. "My heart sank for her."

In total, the clerk allegedly took $446,000 over the last 7 years. "It started relatively small from what we can see, and then just grew into something really big," Bolderson said.

Police say they're working closely with the diocese. *KMBC 9News* says the church has also changed policies to keep it from happening again.

Reprinted in accordance with "fair use" guidelines.

Commentary: Throughout this case, the representative stressed that all parishes in the diocese are required to have a finance council to provide oversight.

A member of that council uncovered a string of false checks. The parish used a checkbook system from which checks were torn out and an accounting stub was left in the book. The employee was writing checks to herself then entering the names of various vendors on the stubs.

***

ChurchMilitant.com
June 9, 2016

Brothers Steal Nearly $1M from Catholic School, Diocese Won't Press Charges*
By Rodney Pelletier

EL PASO, TX (ChurchMilitant.com) — The diocese of El Paso is giving two religious brothers a pass on stealing over $800,000 from the Catholic school they worked in for 25 years.

Brothers Edwin Gallagher and Richard Fish, both members of the Brothers of the Poor of St. Francis (the Order), were the principal and assistant principal at St. Joseph School in El Paso, Texas. An audit performed by the school after the brothers retired in 2015 showed they spent $800,246 out of the school's general fund over seven years. Diocesan officials admit the money was spent without approval from the school board, the pastor, or the diocese. Two more audits performed by the diocese and the Order confirm the findings and show that even more money could be missing going back more than seven years.

In Texas, theft of over $200,000 is a first degree felony punishable by up to 99 years in prison and a $10,000 fine. But the diocese claims it is not pressing charges, maintaining the brothers immediately admitted to it when asked and that they are not employees of the diocese.

The superior of the Brothers of the Poor of St. Francis, based in Cincinnati, is agreeing to pay the diocese back quarterly in $200,000 increments, starting on June 30.

The diocese is not disclosing exactly how the men spent the money. The San Diego Tribune is reporting diocesan spokeswoman, Elizabeth O'Hara, said, "These were not things that men who took a vow of poverty would spend money on," adding that the two men were "beloved" in the community. "It doesn't appear that the brothers intended to commit a crime. They weren't hiding what they were doing."

KVIA in El Paso is reporting "the diocese agreed not to reveal what the money was used for, so it could get the money back from the Order."

O'Hara told ChurchMilitant.com KVIA's comment is "inaccurate" and a "misquote," saying, "Our not talking about the expenditures is not tied to the restitution." She confirmed the decision to keep the brothers' spending secret was made by El Paso bishop Mark Seitz, expressing, "He felt like it was a better opportunity for the diocese to say it was personal expenses."

On Tuesday, Bp. Seitz and diocesan officials met with parishioners at the school gym to disclose the theft to parents, school staff, and community members. He defended the brothers, saying:

Everyone at St. Joseph and many in El Paso know that during that time, they (Gallagher and Fish) did many good things for the school and for the children who study here, and those good things certainly cannot be denied. Unfortunately, we've also learned during that time, or at least a good part of the time, St. Joseph school funds were misappropriated for their own personal use.

A press release by the diocese reads:

The discovery of the misappropriated funds by trusted individuals has caused disappointment and justifiable anger. We are thankful that St. Joseph School will not suffer the adverse financial consequences that accompany most cases of this nature. And we ask for prayers for Brother Edwin and Brother Richard during this Year of Mercy.

An El Paso County District Attorney (D.A.) spokesperson is confirming to ChurchMilitant.com the DA's office and the El Paso Police Department are investigating, but admit it is still too early to know anything.

*Reprinted with permission from *ChurchMilitant.com.*

Commentary: Brother Gallagher and Brother Fish provided more than 25 years of teaching and administrative service to St. Joseph elementary school. Both were much loved and respected for their work.

The two Brothers of the Poor agreed to reimburse the school for the missing money. After the case ended, the school implemented new accounting software with safeguards to prevent future misuse of school funds.

***

Nuns Embezzle $500,000 for Vegas Gambling Trips*
December 17, 2018

Sisters Mary Margaret Kreuper and Lana Chang believed to have siphoned off cash from tuition fees and donations at St James school in Torrance.

Two Catholic nuns have admitted to embezzling $500,000 from a parochial school in Torrance, California. Officials believe the two spent most of the money on travel and casino gambling.

"It is with much sadness that I am informing families of St. James School that an internal investigation has revealed that, over a period of years, Sister Mary Margaret Kreuper and Sister Lana Chang have been involved in the personal use of a substantial amount of School funds," Monsignor Michael Meyers wrote in a letter dated Nov. 28.

Meyers said both nuns acknowledged the theft when confronted, apologized, and were cooperating with an investigation. He said they and their order, the Sisters of St. Joseph of Carondelet, had promised to pay back the money.

Archdiocese officials said they would not be pursuing criminal charges against the women, who retired earlier this year from the school and allegedly expressed remorse for their actions. According to local media reports, parents at the school were angry with the decision, and the outcry compelled the archdiocese to reverse course.

Sgt. Ronald Harris of the Torrance Police Department told the Southern California News Group that archdiocese officials met with police last Thursday.

"They indicated they were desirous of pressing charges, so we're moving forward as soon as we formally meet with them again," Harris told the outlet.

*Composite article based upon stories reported in the 12/10/18 issue of the *Huffington Press,* the 12/11/18 issue of *The Guardian,* and the 12/17/18 issue of *People.com.*

Commentary: The archdiocese indicated the nuns would make complete restitution of the stolen money to St. James School. The pair traveled extensively and claimed they had been given the money by a rich relative.

CHAPTER FOURTEEN
Flood Gates Open in Michigan
2014-2018

During a three-and-a-half-year span, from December 2014 to March 2018, six notable cases surfaced in the Michigan media. Each case had its own identity and a life that seemed endless.

With storylines emerging on a regular basis from the major metropolitan areas across the state — Detroit, Flint, Grand Rapids, Kalamazoo, and Lansing — the issue of priest thievery hit nearly every home. Reading like episodes in a *soap opera*, stories about how they spent the money replicated; sometimes multiple cases appeared on the same newscast.

The cases for Father Kane, Belcazk, Fisher, and Katcher were reported in previous chapters, are not detailed, again. Little information is included on Father Fritz because charges were dropped. Father Wehrle was also introduced earlier, but because of the scope of his case, extended coverage is focused on him.

The following stories illustrate this intense timeframe in Michigan:

December 15, 2014
> **Reverend Timothy Kane Convicted of Stealing $130,000 from the Now-Discontinued Angel Fund**

December 1, 2015
> **Reverend Edward Belczak Sentenced to 27 Months in Prison for Stealing $573,000**

October 9, 2016

> **Reverend Fritz Resigned After Gambling Debts and Questionable Parish Financial Transactions** (Dismissed by the Diocese of Lansing; legal charges were dropped.)

April 7, 2017

> **Catholic Diocese of Lansing says Reverend David Fisher, Pastor for 23 Years at St. Joseph Catholic Church, Stole $450,000**

September 20, 2017

> **Reverend Eugene Katcher Could Face up to Four Years in Prison if He is Convicted of Stealing**

***

And then, there was *the case,* that unfolded in virtually every media outlet across Michigan. It started with Father Wehrle being placed on leave. He was charged with embezzling $100,000. It was disclosed he'd spent $1.85M of parish funds on his estate. Later, it was found he'd spent $45,000 on an indoor swimming pool, $63,000 was discovered in the ceiling of his home, and then he was accused of stealing $5M.

May 10, 2017

Catholic Diocese of Lansing*

Statement regarding Father Jonathan Wehrle

Outside auditors have informed the Diocese of Lansing that there is evidence of a possible significant embezzlement at St. Martha Parish in Okemos. While civil authorities investigate, Father Jonathan W. Wehrle will be on administrative leave from his pastorate of the parish. During this time, Father Michael Murray will serve as temporary administrator. Father Wehrle *previously* submitted his retirement, effective June 28, 2017 and Father Murray will become pastor after that date.

*Reprinted from a public news release.

May 16, 2017

Lansing State Journal

Priest Charged with Embezzling $100K*

MASON — A priest from central Michigan has been charged with embezzlement from his church.

The Rev. Jonathan Wayne Wehrle, 66, was arrested at his Williamston home on Saturday, the 39th anniversary of his ordination. Wehrle was charged Monday with embezzlement of $100,000 or more in Mason District Court.

"I've known Father for almost 30 years, he's not a thief and he is not an embezzler," attorney Lawrence Nolan said. "This is a guy who dedicated his life to the Catholic Church."

The Catholic Diocese of Lansing said last week that Wehrle was placed on administrative leave on May 9, during an investigation by independent auditors into possible embezzlement at the St. Martha Parish in Okemos. A statement from the diocese said the possible embezzlement was referred to police.

Nolan said the priest has independent family money, including funds from a recent sale of his mother's home in Jackson County.

Property records show a home owned by Jonathan W. Wehrle and Dorothy I. Wehrle in Jackson County sold for at least $700,000 in March.

Records also show Jonathan W. Wehrle or the Jonathan W. Wehrle Trust has ownership in three Williamston properties, including a nearly $1.5 million home that the priest listed as his address, in court.

*Reprinted with permission of the *Lansing State Journal.*

June 1, 2017

Lansing State Journal

Hearing for Okemos Priest Charged with Embezzlement Delayed*

By Beth LeBlanc

MASON, MI — A hearing to determine whether an Okemos priest will face trial on an embezzlement charge has been postponed.

The hearing for the Rev. Jonathan Wehrle was rescheduled for July 7 during a hearing Thursday in front of 55th District Court Judge Donald Allen. The delay will allow parties more time to examine paperwork.

Wehrle, the founding pastor of St. Martha Parish in Okemos, is charged with embezzlement of $100,000 or more. Police allege he spent more than $1.85 million in parish funds on his Williamston estate.

Investigators confiscated about 40 boxes of financial documents from the parish and Wehrle's home, which will need to be reviewed before Wehrle's hearing.

Wehrle's lawyer, Lawrence Nolan, has said his client has independent family wealth that may explain his nearly $1.5 million Williamston home and real estate transactions in Jackson County and Highlands County, Florida.

*Reprinted with permission from the *Lansing State Journal.*

July 5, 2017

Lansing State Journal

Okemos Priest Accused of Embezzlement Could Lose $1.4 Million Home*

By Beth LeBlanc

Local prosecutors have filed paperwork to seize the home of a priest charged with stealing from his Okemos parish.

The June 26 filing lists Rev. Jonathan Wehrle's more than $1.4 million home in Williamston and a vacant parcel nearby as subject to civil forfeiture.

*Reprinted with permission from the *Lansing State Journal*.

November 17, 2017

Lansing State Journal

Okemos Priest Will Stand Trial in St. Martha's Embezzlement*

By Beth LeBlanc

MASON, MI -- The Rev. Jonathan Wehrle was bound over by District Judge Donald Allen Friday at the conclusion of a four-day preliminary examination. Wehrle will stand trial on six counts of embezzlement of $100,000 plus.

*Reprinted with permission from the *Lansing State Journal*.

March 30, 2018

Lansing State Journal

Michigan Priest Accused of Embezzlement Sued*

MASON — A Michigan priest accused of embezzling more than $5 million now faces a civil lawsuit filed by the insurance company for the Catholic Diocese of Lansing.

Rev. Jonathan Wehrle is charged with six counts of embezzling $100,000 or more from St. Martha Church in Okemos, east of Lansing. The charges allege Wehrle used the money to pay for home construction, maintenance, and other personal purchases.

On Wednesday a judge approved the Princeton Excess and Surplus Lines Insurance Corporation's request to place Wehrle's more than $1 million estate into receivership. The insurance provider says it's paid out about $2.5 million.

*Reprinted with permission from the *Lansing State Journal.*

July 10, 2018
MICHIGAN RADIO

Nonprofit is Fundraising to Help Lansing-based Priest Accused of Embezzling $5 Million*

According to Michigan Radio, the Catholic organization serves as an advocate for priests in need of legal or personal help — including those accused of embezzling huge amounts of money from their parish.

Catholic non-profit Opus Bono Sacerdotii has begun fundraising for Lansing-area priest Father Jonathan Wehrle's legal and living expenses following last year's allegations that Wehrle embezzled over $5,000,000 from his church.

According to the accusations, Wehrle — who founded St. Martha Parish in Okemos in 1988 — used church money for personal expenses from 1991 to 2017. He now faces federal embezzlement charges, as well as a separate civil suit raised by an insurer for the Catholic Diocese of Lansing.

Wehrle's legal fees are estimated to amount to $300,000, said Michigan Radio. His assets have been frozen while he awaits trial.

*Reprinted according to "fair use" guidelines.

July 18, 2018

Lansing State Journal

Police: $63K Found Stashed Above the Ceiling in Priest's Basement*

By Ken Palmer

WILLIAMSTON, MI - Police said they found more than $63,000 in cash during a second search of the home of a Catholic priest charged with embezzling more than $5 million from an Okemos parish.

The money was found above ceiling tiles in the basement of the Rev. Jonathan Wehrle's lavish home on Noble Road, Michigan State Police said Wednesday in a news release.

*Reprinted with permission of the *Lansing State Journal.*

August 2, 2018

WILX 10

LANSING, Mich. (WILX) — The lawyer representing a priest charged with embezzlement is withdrawing from the case.

During a hearing on Wednesday, Larry Nolan, of Nolan, Thomsen & Villas, told an Ingham County Circuit Court judge he intends to end his defense of Father Jonathan Wehrle.

Attorneys Joe Poprawa and John Fraser of Grewal Law will take over.

Wehrle is charged with six counts of embezzling more than $100,000 from St. Martha parish in Okemos. Auditors say the parish is missing more than $5 million. Investigators have seized around $1 million from Wehrle. They say they found more than $60,000 cash in the ceiling tiles of his multi-million-dollar home near Williamston.

*Reprinted with permission from WLIX.

A satellite image and pictures of the Wehrle estate follow in Figures 1 – 4.

Figure 1 — The Wehrle 10 Acre-Estate
(Courtesy of Google Earth Link)

Figure 2 – Front Entrance of Wehrle Estate
(Courtesy of Michigan State Police)

146

Figure 3 – Lakeside View of Wehrle Estate
(Courtesy of Michigan State Police)

Figure 4 – Indoor Swimming Pool — Wehrle Estate
(Courtesy of Michigan State Police)

Lansing State Journal
August 1, 2018

Priest to Get New Attorneys: Embezzlement Trial Pushed Back to 2019*
By Christopher Haxel

LANSING, MI — The trial for a retired priest accused of stealing more than $5 million from a Roman Catholic parish in Okemos is delayed until at least January because his attorney plans to withdraw from the case.

The Rev. Jonathan Wehrle is expected to have new legal representation soon, although the switch has not yet been formalized.

Lawrence Nolan, his current attorney, told the State Journal he planned to withdraw from the case shortly after Michigan State Police announced in July, they found more than $63,000 in cash hidden in the ceiling of his home.

The retired priest's trial on six felony counts of embezzlement of $100,000 or more had been set for later this month, but Judge Joyce Draganckuk on Wednesday scheduled a new start date of Jan. 7.

Speaking at a hearing in Ingham County Circuit Court, Draganckuk said an October trial would not give Wehrle's attorneys enough time to prepare, given the voluminous paperwork associated with the case,

Joseph Poprawa and John Fraser of Grewal Law PLLC in Okemos said after the hearing that they've been retained by Wehrle.

Michigan State Police last month said they found $63,392 in Wehrle's home after receiving information from Lansing Police. The bundles of bills were wrapped in paper bands stamped with the words: "For deposit only — St. Martha Parish and School," police said. Other evidence related to the investigation also was seized, although police did not specify what that evidence includes.

*Reprinted with permission of the Lansing State Journal.

Commentary: The case against the clergyman in this story is going to trial in 2019. It's a classic case of an overly trusting environment with a highly manipulative fraudster and ineffective oversight. Few controls existed over Wehrle's handling of church money. He was able to write checks to himself without receipts and regularly take entire Sunday collections, while the Catholic Diocese of Lansing, Michigan failed to ask serious questions.

CHAPTER FIFTEEN
The Gathering Storm

With the end of another decade drawing near, the hierarchy of the Catholic Church remained steadfast in the past. Pope Francis has an eye toward the future, but it seems as if he has the weight of a giant organizational boulder on his shoulders. The sex abuse scandal moves into its sixteenth year with no end in sight. Evidence of Church cultural decay appears as the unabated thievery scandal reaches into the Vatican. Responses to a growing number of issues moves at the pace of a dinosaur — leaving some to wonder if the out-of-touch Church will face the same fate.

Catholic News Agency
May 9, 2018

Embezzlement Trial Begins for Ex-Vatican Bank President*

Vatican City, May 9, 2018 / 10:25 am (CNA/EWTN News) — According to the *Catholic News Agency,* the first hearing in a trial against the former president of the *Institute of Religious Works (IOR) – known as the "Vatican Bank" –* and his lawyer took place today at the Vatican.

Court records indicated Angelo Caloia, 78, president of the IOR from 1989-2009 and his lawyer, Gabriele Liuzzo, 95, were indicted March 5 on accusations of having embezzled money from Vatican real estate sales during the years 2001-2008.

At the hearing May 9, the Vatican Court announced plans to appoint experts who will assess the value of properties that Caloia and Liuzzo are accused of selling at below-market

rates — while allegedly making off-paper agreements for higher amounts to pocket the difference. The amount embezzled is estimated to be 57 million euros ($68 million).
*Reprinted in accordance with "fair use" guidelines.

Commentary: This case confirms the belief of many that devious actions permeate the Church. Certainly, the effects of this financial misconduct at the highest level will likely linger long into the future.

***

Independent.co.UK
November 12, 2018

Vatican Orders US Bishops to Postpone Crucial Vote on Sexual Abuse Crisis*
By Sarah Harvard, New York

According to *Independent.com,* the Vatican has instructed US Catholic bishops to postpone plans to vote on proposed new steps to address the clergy sex abuse crisis embroiling the church.

The US Conference of Catholic Bishops (USCCB) was planning to vote on a referendum that would hold bishops responsible for failing to protect children from sexual abuse in the church, *Independent.com* stated.

In an announcement to his fellow Catholic clergymen, USCCB President Cardinal Daniel DiNardo said the Holy See requested the conference to hold off their vote until February when the Vatican will hold their global meeting on sexual abuse.

"We are not, ourselves, happy about this," Mr. DiNardo said, with much chagrin, at a press conference in Baltimore on Monday morning. "We have been working hard to get to the action stage, and we'll do it, but we have to get past this bump in the road."

Mr. DiNardo said he was made aware of the decision on Sunday.

Shortly after Mr. DiNardo's announcement, Archbishop Christopher Pierre, the Vatican's ambassador to the United States, argued bishops should not be held responsible for non-ordained members of the church and should not have to seek assistance from law enforcement to tackle the sexual abuse epidemic.
*Reprinted in accordance with "fair use" guidelines.

Commentary: The last sentence of the Vatican ambassador's statement is critical — "should not have to seek assistance from law enforcement..." Is this a call for leaders to close ranks and keep issues inside the Church? Does it suggest the Pope may have a sense how many priests could ultimately be involved? Does it suggest that if these cases were handled in the courts, they would break the bank?

***

Impact of Unreported Thievery Cases

Still, church officials can no longer ignore the skyrocketing costs of the thievery scandal. Stealing is not just a rumor joked about around the coffee pot. It's not one person taking 15 or 20 dollars from a collection plate or a secretary cheating on a deposit slip — it's planned, systematic theft by a trusted, long time employees that's costing the Church over a billion dollars every year.

Regarding this point, Barry Bowen (2) indicated earlier in chapter 8, a point that bears repeating:

> One of the dirty secrets of Christianity is that there are numerous crooked pastors, priests, and church financial secretaries embezzling funds. The International Bulletin of Missionary Research projected that $37 billion would be stolen by Christian religious leaders in 2013 and this fraud will reach $60 billion by 2025.

The $37B mentioned above is for all Christian churches, worldwide. Using the guides described by Johnson, Zurlo, and

Hickman (12) in their defining article, "Embezzlement in the Global Christian Community," it was determined the amount of fraud for the Catholic churches in the U.S. resulted in funds stolen from the Church in 2013 to be estimated at $803M. The model was then used to provide estimates for the following years, as illustrated in Chart 14.

ESTIMATED DOLLAR STOLEN	
Year	U.S. Catholic Church
2014	$.955B
2015	$1.107B
2016	$1.194B
2017	$1.237B
2018	$1.261B
Total	$5.754B

Chart 14 — Estimated Dollars Stolen from the Catholic Church

The projections by Johnson and others have been amazingly accurate over the years. Still, to ensure their accuracy, the projected losses were validated by comparisons made by using data from the "2018 Report to the Nations," issued by the Association of Certified Fraud Examiners. The disparity between the two approaches was insignificant.

With the financial fallout of the sex abuse scandal exceeding $3B and the losses due to thievery projected to increase from $1.261B to $1.3B in 2019, the burden on the Church's financial bottom line is unprecedented. The shortfall is increasing at a staggering rate.

Summary of Costs for the Notable Cases

The 97 notable cases of $100,000 or more used in this report are only a small piece of the pie, but they provide examples of how thievery occurs daily in the Church. And, all of this because the Church is unwilling to move beyond a medieval set of definitions — where bishops are beyond reproach, priests have complete latitude in managing the parish, and both have unchecked custodial and visionary responsibilities.

As visionaries, the priests are godly. They provide religious services and preach the Gospel. Unlike Protestants, who typically separate the oversight of finances with the laity, the priests are custodians and business managers with potentially unchecked control over parish finances.

Further, the increased cost of notable cases summarized in Chart 15 illustrates how a few can take advantage of the church's archaic system and use money donated for religious causes for their own purposes.

The chart puts into perspective how the total amount of dollars stolen in notable cases skyrocketed from 2002 to 2018 with the last case bursting onto the national scene December 7, 2018.

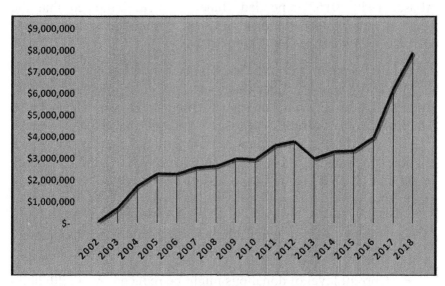

Chart 15 — Tip of the Iceberg

It's instructive to characterize the spiraling amount of lost dollars in the notable cases as the tip of an iceberg. By using the 2018 losses of $7,932,000 from chart 15 as the divisor and the 2018 estimated losses of $1.261B from chart 14 as the dividend, it is possible to gain a better perspective of the magnitude of the dollars stolen annually from Catholic churches in the U.S.

($1.261B divided by $7.932M = 160)

It's a staggering relationship — if the chart above represented the tip of a real iceberg, the size of the submerged part would be roughly 160 times larger than the tip.

(Remember, these are dollars given by parishioners in good faith, for a specific purpose, NOT for the personal aggrandizement of a thief.)

Potential Financial Impact of the Sex Abuse Scandal

While this research is focused on the thievery scandal, one cannot ignore the potential financial impact of the sex abuse scandal. The "Collated USCCB Data: On the Number of U. S. Priests Accused of Sexually Abusing Children and the Number of Persons Alleging Abuse, 1950-2016," amended, June 1, 2018, indicated that the USCCB now projects "priests might have molested well in excess of 100,000 children in the United States."

That's five times more than the number of victims identified thus far. Many of these are older cases and may not be pursued legally. But should the Church continue to muddle its way through the handling of only half of these cases — 50,000 individuals — that's two and a half times more than the number that have come forward, it's hard to imagine the consequences the U.S. Catholic Church might face. It could result in the loss of billions of dollars. Could it mean the:

- Number of Lapsed Catholics might increase by another 10M, 20M or 30M?

- Current level of donations might be reduced by 10, 20, or 30 percent?

- $3B already paid out for sex abuse compensation might escalate to $10B or more?

These possibilities and the resulting fallout make it clear Church officials must take substantive corrective action to *stop this lanced cancerous boil from spilling more venomous poison.*

Catholic Church Under Siege

The Pope is under fire.

The poorly managed sex abuse scandal is on the verge of exploding — with thousands of cases ready to come to light. From the thievery scandal, $5.7B has been stolen from the Church in the past five years — *nearly doubling the $3B paid out in major sex abuse cases.* For the first time in centuries, pressure is growing on the Catholic Church — there's a multitude of forces — anyone with the potential to create unparalleled change!

Sex Abuse Scandal. As the driving force, the demand for greater openness and transparency generated by the sex abuse scandal cannot be tossed aside. One way or another — from the Church, from a legal perspective, from media and/or the membership — changes are in the offering.

Thievery Scandal. The amount of thievery in the Church — embezzlement, fraud, money laundering, stealing — increased significantly throughout the century. Each case strikes a new chord with the media, increasing the likelihood that the next story will receive more airtime. The $1.3B projected to be stolen in 2019 will likely surpass the amount of new costs in the sex abuse scandal, making *church thievery the biggest ongoing scandal* in the country.

Faith-based Organization. For individuals outside the Church, this seems like an easy challenge to address: simply move beyond the archaic "faith-based organization" model to adopt a more contemporary "faith/business-based organization" that separates the flow of dollars from the ministry and makes individuals at every level accountable. But… will that happen?

Michigan Thievery Cases. The cases in Michigan present two challenges for the Church. First, the cases are against multiple priests scattered across the state, which makes it a statewide issue. Any blip, big or small, has the potential of igniting a firestorm that could spread state-to-state. Second, the $5M Wehrle case will no doubt *keep the fires of discontentment burning.* It's already grabbed national attention and will garner continued monitoring by all the major media outlets.

Disconnections. Society and cultural values have changed; the Church remains recalcitrant. The issues are many — abortion, homosexuality, priest celibacy, women priests — to name a few. All religions must answer to a higher power — the people — the world's oldest, wealthiest, and most powerful church is *NOT* infallible.

Church Financial Problems. The Church is dealing with financial issues on virtually every front — decaying churches with huge maintenance costs, underfunded priest pensions, new churches needed in the south and west, and worse, the closing of parishes and dwindling weekly donations. These make the worst possible combination — rising costs and revenue losses.

Embezzlement at the Vatican. Typically, problems at the Vatican have had little impact on the rest of the world, but the embezzlement of $62M by the former president of the Vatican Bank adds fodder to the thievery issue. It indicates corruption is present at all levels of the Church and gives credence to those who believe it's time for change.

The Pope's Actions. While popular in the polls, the pope added fuel to the firestorm when he stopped the U.S. bishops from acting on a set of U.S. Conference of Catholic Bishops proposals on how to deal with allegations against bishops.

Actions by State Attorneys General. The attorneys general in Pennsylvania and Illinois have released reports implicating hundreds of sex abuse cases against priests in their states, which resulted in a public outcry for the bishops to act. Twelve other State AGs are in the process of taking similar action. The attorney general in Michigan has opened what is defined on the State website as an "independent, thorough, transparent, and prompt," investigation into "what's happened within the Catholic Church."

Lawsuits in California. Two recently filed federal lawsuits from sex abuse victims are far more sweeping than individual cases against priests in the past. One is utilizing the RICO Act (Racketeer Influenced and Corrupt Organizations Act), originally conceived to take down drug dealers and the mafia. It aims to force U.S. bishops to divulge secret lists of offenders dating back more than six decades. The other blames Vatican officials for misconduct in the United States.

Using the RICO Act, the first case focuses on sex offenders, but will undoubtedly include priest thievery that accompanied their atrocities — and if that happens, all cases of thievery are potential targets. The other one relies on nuisance laws, alleging the Church has created a public hazard. It, too, has the potential of raising broad-based issues, something the Church certainly doesn't want.

The Brewing Storm

On December 29, 2018, CNN Religious Editor Daniel Burke (4) summarized the year in an article, "How 2018 Became the Catholic Church's Year from Hell." Prior to detailing the year, month-by-month, he made several salient points:

> A prominent cardinal resigned in disgrace. Grand jurors accused hundreds of Catholic clerics of secretly abusing children. A former Vatican ambassador urged the pope himself, to step down.

> It was enough for New York's Cardinal Timothy Dolan to call it the Catholic Church's "summer of…"

> … the church's hellish year began in January, when Pope Francis forcefully defended a Chilean bishop he had promoted. He later had to apologize and accept the bishop's resignation.

> … the sex abuse scandal shows no signs of abating, with a federal investigation and probes in 12 states and the District of Columbia in the works.

> "The Catholic Church cannot police itself," said Lisa Madigan, Illinois' attorney general, in announcing that Catholic leaders had withheld the names of 500 clergy members accused of abuse.

> The church's institutional crisis is mirrored by individual soul-searching, as American Catholics question whether to stay in the church. 2018 saw parents challenging priests at Mass, prominent Catholics urging the faithful to withhold

donations, and parents worrying for their children's safety in the sacristy.

One Catholic historian called it the church's greatest crisis since the 1517 Reformation.

***

As overwhelming as these issues might seem, the Church's mission of faith will sustain its continuance, but how will it re-achieve its momentum? Will church officials take corrective actions that address the immediate problem? Or, will church officials make systemic changes that will affect the operation of the entire church?

Mindful of these issues, a reflective thought back to 2009 provides an interesting perspective on the Church's future. At the time, General Motors embodied one of America's greatest success stories. It had grown from a small shop to become a super-corporation producing stellar automobiles — Buicks, Cadillacs, Oldsmobiles, Pontiacs, Camaros, and Corvettes — it was a world-renowned success story!

Experts agreed across-the-board, "General Motors is too big to fail."

But...IT DID!

Comparison Between:
General Motors in 2009 Catholic Church in 2019

STAGGERING LEGACY COSTS

Worker retirement costs	Religious retirement costs
Health care costs	Health care costs
Antiquated auto plants	Decaying churches
Poorly located auto plants	Poorly attended "inner city" churches

STANDARDS AND EXPECTATIONS

Fuel economy requirements	Ban on married clergy
Focus on big cars & trucks	Ignore thievery scandal
Slow to get in step with changes	Unwilling to act openly
Poor design & interiors	Failure to seek & apply lay input

LESS THAN STELLAR PRODUCTS

Market share fell	Lapsed & departed Catholics
Chevy Vega	Priestly celibacy
Citation	Abortion & contraception
Chevette	LGBTQ acceptance

A GROUP OF TRADITIONAL ELITEST

Bloated upper management	Vatican "deadwood" haven
Obsessed with numbers	Out-of-touch hierarchy
"Bean-counter" mentality	Asking for more money
Lack of creativity/unwillingness to change	Insulated Vatican traditionalist

The parallels between General Motors and the Catholic Church are startling. The Catholic Church may not *fail* in a traditional sense — *the Catholic religion will continue — it must eliminate its archaic practices of the past* if it is to stop its decline in membership and recapture the trust of its parishioners.

Without specific direction from the Pope, it's difficult to imagine how the Church's internal operations will allow it to be a viable entity. The Church must move forward with a sense of urgency, if it to avoid the most dreaded question of all:

Is the Catholic Church too big to fail?

Epilogue

Pope Declares Rare Decree: Action will Implement "Faith-Based/Business" Policy to Eliminate Thievery

UNITED STATES — Pope Francis set aside five hundred years of history, when he announced a new "Faith-Based/Business" policy. In a nationally televised speech given to the U.S. Conference of Catholic Bishops, the Pope redefined how parishes and dioceses would handle financial matters.

Referring to the $1.2 billion stolen annually in the U.S., the Pope told the bishops, "You were called upon to address 21st Century issues within a medieval framework — that must change! There are many priests and parishes where this cancerous thievery has been allowed to flourish — that must change!"

(What if this headline was in the newspaper the day after Pope Francis delivered such a speech? If it happened, here's the type of speech he might have given.)

Dear Brother Bishops,

I am pleased we can meet at this point in the apostolic mission which has brought me to your country. I thank the two cardinals to my right for making the arrangements for the live telecast of my remarks to every city in this vast land.

As I look out with affection at you, and your pastors in the parishes, I would ask you to share my affection and spiritual closeness with the People of God throughout this wonderful country.

The heart of the Pope expands to include everyone. But today, I come to you with a heavy heart. For centuries a cancer has been growing in the bowels of the Church. Unknowingly, we have allowed it to develop its own sub-culture —one of ethical misconduct and one in which *thievery has become the accepted norm* for some of those in the Vatican and those in leadership positions throughout the world.

In my few years in Rome, I have heard many stories of atrocities *not only against mankind, but those against individuals* who had dedicated their lives and souls to the Church. We are aware of abuses of power and cover-ups of immoralities that are all too often the norm. No longer can we sit on the side idly; we must engage in productive dialogue that defines the priesthood in a way that these practices are no longer a part of us.

When I was young, I recall my mother placing the few pennies she had in the collection plate, and then, she'd hear of individuals who'd spent dollars, hundreds of dollars, for their own personal pleasures.

Rumors, innuendos, these realities have plagued us throughout the years. In reading *THIEVERY: Catholic Church EXPOSED!* I have learned those rumors, innuendos, pennies, and dollars are costing the Church in this great nation over $1.2 billion a year. This cancerous thievery must be eradicated from our midst!

I am conscious of the courage with which you have faced difficult moments in this country in the recent history of the Church, without fear of criticism and at the cost of mortification and great sacrifice. Often, I am afraid, you were not given the latitude to do what needed to be done, nor were you given the tools to achieve your purposes.

You were called upon to address 21st Century issues within a medieval framework — that must change!

We are bishops of the Church, shepherds appointed by God to lead his flock. Our greatest joy is to be shepherds — and only shepherds — pastors with undivided hearts and selfless devotion. We need to preserve this joy and never let ourselves be robbed of it.

There are a few priests and parishes where this cancerous growth has been allowed to flourish — that must change!

You have been afraid to take whatever actions were necessary to regain the authority and trust which is demanded of ministers of Christ and rightly expected by the faithful. You need not be afraid; we must assure all parishioners that no longer will $1.2 billion be used inappropriately. It "will be used for the intended purposes!"

I speak to you as the Bishop of Rome, called by God in old age, to watch over the unity of the universal Church and to encourage in charity the journey of all toward ever greater knowledge, faith, and love of Christ.

Often, I have said, "I have no wish to tell you what to do, because we all know what it is that the Lord asks of us." But, today, I come to you with a plan and implementation strategies. In no way do I come to judge or lecture you; rather, it's a new path for us to take and the spirit with which we need to work.

I repeat— "it's a new path for us to take and the spirit with which we need to work!"

We must replace the closed, secretive doctrine of medieval days with openness as clear as the sky above. Dialogue is our method, not as a shrewd strategy, but out of fidelity to the One who never wearies of our visits.

The path ahead, then, is dialogue among yourselves, dialogue with your presbyters, dialogue with lay persons, dialogue with families, dialogue with society. I will never tire of encouraging you to dialogue fearlessly. The keys to the future are communication, accountability, and transparency.

Again, I cannot state too boldly — "the keys to the future are communication, accountability, and transparency!"

We must accept the responsibility for the thievery that's occurred over the years and acknowledge that it rests at our feet. First, as Pope and those who preceded me, we failed to ensure donations made to the Church were used for their intended purposes; and second, those of you in the audience and the bishops before you failed to ensure donations made to the Church were used for their intended purposes.

Without claiming to be exhaustive, I will share with you the essence of the plan, which will be further defined in future communications:

We are a "faith-based" church, but we cannot operate the church with "blind faith." We must recognize the failings of a few within us and take advantage of sound business practices that will prevent those souls who might be tempted to steal.

Our actions must ensure that separation of duties is practiced at every stage, so there is always more than one person engaged in each financial step. A diocesan audit of each parish must be conducted no less than every three years. Opportunities for thievery must be held to a minimum, with a limited number of credit cards and bank accounts as well as controls in place to ensure that checks and balances are in place for every transaction.

With the "Faith-Based/Business" Policy I'm announcing today, each of you will be accountable for the implementation of "all USCCB policies and procedures in each of the parishes reporting to you." And if it is found that every financial policy is not fully implemented in a parish, enabling full transparency, the bishop will share responsibility for such inaction.

I repeat — "the bishop will share responsibility for such inaction!"

Bishops will be accountable for the oversight of each parish in the diocese/archdiocese to ensure the parish conducts annual reports, the financial council is functioning effectively and is composed of a majority of members with financial expertise, and open communications are maintained with the parishioners.

Priests will be accountable for the operation of USCCB policies and procedures in the parish. That means they will be accountable for ensuring that everyone — the business manager, secretary, members of the financial committee, etc. — employ sound business/ management practices. And, they will annually verify to the bishop that each USCCB procedure has been effectively implemented. Failure to implement, manage, and follow such protocols will be "grounds for dismissal."

Bishops must have the farsightedness of a leader and demonstrate the shrewdness of a wise administrator; otherwise, we risk a fall into hopeless decline. The Church is torn and divided; brokenness is now everywhere. Consequently, the Church, "the seamless garment of the Lord," cannot allow herself to be rented, broken, or fought over.

Our mission as bishops is first and foremost to solidify unity, a unity whose content is defined by the Word of God and the one Bread of Heaven. Still, the church does not function in isolation. We are part of a community of those like us and those unlike us. There are times when we must reach out to those in the legal system.

I'm reluctant to tell you, but I feel I must. When a potential case of fraud, embezzlement, or any other form of thievery comes to your attention, you must utilize the legal avenues available in your great country. And, if you don't report the misconduct, should the same issue become public in any form, you will personally share in the blame.

These essential aspects of the Church's mission belong to the core of what we have received from the Lord. We must preserve and communicate them. We must find ways to encourage spiritual growth, to protect the interest of the parishioners. We must ensure dollars entrusted to us are dedicated to the holy purposes of the church for which they were intended.

May God bless you and Our Lady watch over you!

---

*This statement is an adaptation of Pope Francis' speech to the US Bishops on September 23, 2015—all references to thievery have been added. Many of these suggestions for reform are based on the referenced writings of Paul Gorrell, a former priest; Michael W. Ryan, a retired federal investigator concerned about lax cash-handling in U.S. parishes; and Charles Zech, a tireless advocate for implementing sound money-management procedures, at the Center for Church Management, Villanova University.

This "draft" speech was mailed by author Les Cochran to Pope Francis on September 5, 2019.

The Author's Writings

Les Cochran is a historical fiction author, who diverted his energies, between scholarly efforts, to research nearly two decades of Catholic Church history to produce *THIEVERY: Catholic Church EXPOSED!* Prior to writing his first three books in his *Detroit Thorn Birds Defy Mafia* series and his *Love,* Lies, *and Liaisons* trilogy, Dr. Cochran produced four professional books, over fifty academic articles and numerous guest opinions. Now retired, he culminated his academic career as President of Youngstown State University. For more information go to www.LesCochran.com.

Detroit Thorn Birds Defy Mafia Series

SAX CLUB: *Detroit Thorn Birds Defy Mafia*

BLIND PIG: *Detroit Thorn Birds Defy Mafia*

GET EVEN: *Detroit Thorn Birds Defy Mafia*

Love, Lies and Liaisons Trilogy

SIGNATURE AFFAIR: *Love, Lies and Liaisons*

COSTLY AFFAIR: *Love, Lies and Liaisons*

PRESIDENTAIL AFFAIR: *Love, Lies and Liaisons*

* * *

Join the author's "Friends and Fans" at:
www.LesCochranBlog.com.

Bibliography

(1)   Allen, Jr., "The Deep Pockets, The Butler Did It, and Myths About Atheism," **National Catholic Reporter**. August 17, 2012.

(2)   Bowen, Barry, "How to Spot a Pastor or Priest Stealing Church Funds," **Time for Everything**. June 3, 2013.

(3)   Bowen, Barry, "Religious Financial Fraud: Balance Sheet for Global Christianity," excerpt in **Pulpit&Pen.** July 7, 2017.

(4)   Briggs, David, "The Financial Crisis Facing U. S. Churches," **Huffington Press**. November 6, 2016.

(5)   Burke, Daniel, "How 2018 Became the Catholic Church's Year from Hell," **CNN**. December 29, 2018.

(6)   Byers, Larry and Hurlburt, Greg (2004), "Embezzlement – it can happen to you!" Retrieved from http://www.byershurlburtcpa.com/Articles7.htm. September 21, 2005.

(7)   Canavan, Brendan, "Catholicism's Multi-billion Brand is Struggling Despite Pope Francis," **The Conversation**. April 18, 2016.

(8)   "Catholic Church in the United States," **Wikipedia.org.** Undated.

(9)   "Catholic Priest," **allaboutrelegion.org.** Undated.

(10) "Collated USCCB Data: On the Number of U. S. Priests Accused of Sexually Abusing Children and the Number of Persons Alleging Abuse, 1950-2016," amended, **Bishopaccountability.org**. June 1, 2018.

(11) "Early Concerns—The Catholic Church in America," **The Economist**. August 18, 2012.

(12) "Diocesan Internal Controls: A Framework," A Paper Printed by the U.S. Conference of Catholic Bishops, 1995.

(13) "Diocesan Financial Issues," A Document Developed by the Committee on Budget and Finance. USCCB, November 2002.

(14) "158th Diocesan Convention Passes 9 Resolutions, Elects 29 Offices," **Pacific Church News**. December 2007.

(15) "Embezzlement: The Secret Hidden in God's House," **PraiseBuilding.com**. February 8, 2013.

(16) Feeney, Tom, "Catholic Church Faces Problems of Priest Thefts," **Chicago Tribune**. December 31, 2004.

(17) Feuerherd, Peter, "Secured Collection Systems Protect Parish Funds, Integrity Against Theft," **National Catholic Reporter.** February 2, 2016.

(18) Forney, Bob, "Protecting God's Money: Tips to Prevent Church Embezzlement," **Fraudulent Misappropriation.** May 3, 2018.

(19) Fraga, Brian, "Magazine Profiles Focuses Attention on Church Finances," **OVS Newsweekly.** August 29, 2012.

(20) Gorrell, Paul, "Hands in the Till: When Priests Steal," **Religious Dispatches.** June 19, 2009.

(21) Gjelten, Tom, "The Clergy Abuse Crisis Has Cost the Catholic Church $3 Billion," **npr.org.** August 18, 2018.

(22) Gray, Mark M., Gautier, Mary L., and Cidade, Melissa A., "The Changing Face of U.S. Catholic Parishes," Research Conducted by the Center for Applied research in the Apostolate. 2010.

(23) Hill, Cathy, "Why did General Motors Fail?" **New York Daily News.** May 31, 2010.

(24) Hoge, Dean, McNamara, Patrick, and Zech, Charles. **Plain Talk about Churches and Money.** July 10, 2014.

(25) Johnson, Todd M., Zurlo, Gina A., and Hickman, Albert J., "Embezzlement in the Global Christian Community," **The Review of Faith & International Affairs**. Volume 13, Number 2 (Summer 2015).

(26) Libresco, Leah, "Diversity, Leaky Roofs, and Aging Priests: Inside the Changing U.S. Catholic Church," **American Magazine**. February 1, 2017.

(27) Lotich, Patricia, "18 Shocking Facts About Church Embezzlement," **Sharefaith Magazine.** September 18, 2015.

(28) Lowe, Herbert, "Last Ones to Suspect," **Newsday.com.** July 24, 2005.

(29) McCormick, Bill, "Here's Why the Vatican Stopped American Bishops from Voting on Responses to Sexual Abuse," **The Washington Post.** November 15, 2018.

(30) Morris-Young, Dan, "Study of U.S. Priests: Aging is 'Most Striking Trend,'" **National Catholic Reporter.** March 12, 2012.

(31) McClory, Robert, "Collection Racket," **U.S. Catholic**, Vol. 74, No. 5, May 2009, pages 12-17.

(32) Pavlo, Walter, "Fraud Thriving in U.S. Churches, But You Wouldn't Know It," **Forbes.com.**, November 18, 2013.

(33) "Priest, Bishop Clash in Sex, Theft Scandals," **The Washington Times.** November 12, 2002.

(34) "Priest Pension Crisis: $74M Gap in Retirement Fund," **Boston Herald.** March 20, 2015.

(35) "Religious Financial Fraud: Balance Sheet for Global Christianity," **Pulpit & Pen**. July 2017.

(36) Reuters, "As Pope Visit Nears, US Catholic Church Faces Financial Strain," **New York Post.** September 8, 2015.

(37) Richert, Scott P., "Can a Woman Be a Priest in the Catholic Church?" **Thoughtco.com.** August 7, 2018.

(38) Ryan, Michael W., *NONFEASANCE: The Remarkable Failure of the Catholic Church to Protect Its Primary Source of Income.* Church Revenue Protection, www.ChurchSecurity.info, 2011.

(39) Ryan, Michael W., "The Second Greatest Scandal in the Church," **BishopAccountability.org.** June 15, 2005.

(40) Schnurr, Dennis M., "Parish Financial Governance," A Letter to All Bishops. Washington, D.C.: **U.S. Conference of Catholic Bishops, Finance Office**. March 23, 2007.

(41) Smietana, Bob, "Robbing God, Literally: 1 in 10 Protestant Churches Experience Embezzlement," **Christianitytoday.com.** August 3, 2017.

(42) Smith, Erin, "Priest pension crisis: $74M gap in retirement fund," **Boston Herald.** March 30, 2015.

(43) Skimming (Fraud), **Wikipedia.org.** Undated.

(44) Tokasz, Jay, "Church wrestling with theft prevention, millions stolen nationwide over the last five years," **PressReader.com.** June 2, 2010.

(45) "Top Five Trends in Catholic Church Finances in the 21st Century," Villanova, PA: Center for Church Management & Business Ethic, **Villanova University.** Undated.

(46) Ventura, Melvin and Daniel, Shirley J., "Opportunities for Fraud and Embezzlement in Religious Organizations: An Exploratory Study," **Journal of Forensic & Investigative Accounting.** 2010, Vol. 1, Issue 1.

(47) West, Robert and Zech, Charles, "Internal Financial Controls in the U. S. Catholic Church," A Study Supported by the Louisville Institute, Villanova PA: **Villanova University.** 2007.

(48) "What is a Catholic Priest?" **vocationcentre.org.** Undated.

(49) Winters, Michael Sean, "US Bishops Won't Restore Trust with Announced Plans to Stop Abuse," **National Catholic Reporter.** September 24, 2018.

(50) Zech, Charles, "How to Stop Embezzlement in Your Parish," **U.S. Catholic.org.** January 24, 2017.

(51) Zech, Chuck, "Best Practices in Catholic Parish Internal Financial Controls," Power-point Presentation, **Villanova University: Center for Church Management.** 2018.

Printed by BoD™in Norderstedt, Germany

9 780578 523521